CLAIT Plus 2006

Unit 2
Manipulating Spreadsheets and Graphs

Using
Microsoft® Excel 2007

Release CP652v1

Published by:

CiA Training Ltd
Business & Innovation Centre
Sunderland Enterprise Park
Sunderland SR5 2TH
United Kingdom

Tel: +44 (0)191 549 5002
Fax: +44 (0)191 549 9005

E-mail: info@ciatraining.co.uk
Web: www.ciatraining.co.uk

ISBN 13: 978-1-86005-466-2

Important Note

This guide was written using *Windows Vista* with a screen resolution of 1024 x 768.

Using Windows XP will result in many dialog boxes looking different, although the content is the same.

Working in a different screen resolution, or with an application window which is not maximised, will change the look of the *Office 2007* Ribbon. The ribbon appearance is dynamic, it changes to fit the space available. The full ribbon may show a group containing several options, but if space is restricted it may show a single button that you need to click to see the same options, e.g. the **Editing** group may be replaced by the **Editing** button.

First published 2007

Copyright © 2007 CiA Training Ltd

Excel 2007   CLAIT Plus

CiA Training's guides for CLAIT Plus 2006 are a collection of structured exercises to provide support for each unit in the new qualification. The exercises build into a complete open learning package covering the entire syllabus, to teach how to use particular software applications. They are designed to take the user through the features to enhance, fulfil and instil confidence in the product.

UNIT 2: MANIPULATING SPREADSHEETS AND GRAPHS - The guide supporting this core unit contains exercises covering the following topics.

Spreadsheet Principles	Functions
Screen and Worksheet	Manipulating Workbooks
Task Panes	Creating Charts
Menus	Formatting Charts
Creating a Spreadsheet	Cell Referencing
Saving and Opening	Printing Spreadsheets and Charts
Formatting Worksheets	Sorting and Filtering Data
Editing and Copying	Names
Formulas	Linking

Visit **www.ciasupport.co.uk** for hints, tips and supplementary information on published CiA products.

This guide is suitable for:

- Any individual wishing to sit the OCR examination for this unit. The user works through the guide from start to finish. Some prior knowledge of *Excel 2007* would be useful, gained for example from working through the corresponding units produced by CiA Training for New CLAIT.

- Tutor led groups as reinforcement material. It can be used as and when necessary.

Aims and Objectives

To provide the knowledge and techniques necessary for the attainment of a certificate in this core unit. After completing the guide the user will be able to:

- Create spreadsheets
- Format spreadsheets
- Maintain spreadsheets
- Create and format charts
- Print spreadsheets, formulas and charts

Downloading the Data Files

The data associated with these exercises must be downloaded from our website. Go to: **www.ciatraining.co.uk/data**. Follow the on screen instructions to download the appropriate data files.

By default, the data files will be downloaded to **Documents\CIA DATA FILES\CLAIT Plus 2006\Unit 2 Excel 2007 Data**.

If you prefer, the data can be supplied on CD at an additional cost. Contact the Sales team at **info@ciatraining.co.uk**.

Introduction

This guide was created using *Excel 2007*. It assumes that the program has been correctly and **fully** installed on your personal computer. Some features described in this guide may not work if the program was not **fully** installed.

Important Notes For All Users

The downloaded data accompanying this guide contains files to enable the user to practise new techniques without the need for data entry. Newly created files can be saved to the same location.

Notation Used Throughout This Guide

- Key presses are included within < > e.g. <**Enter**> means press the Enter key.

- The guide is split into individual exercises. Each exercise consists of a written explanation of the feature, followed by a stepped exercise. Read the **Guidelines** and then follow the **Actions**, with reference to the **Guidelines** if necessary.

Recommendations

- Work through the exercises in sequence so that one feature is understood before moving on to the next.

- Read the whole of each exercise before starting to work through it. This ensures the understanding of the topic and prevents unnecessary mistakes.

Section 1

Creating a Spreadsheet

By the end of this Section you should be able to:

Understand Spreadsheet Structure

Create a New Spreadsheet

Enter Numbers and Labels

Save a Workbook

Close a Workbook

Exercise 1 - Spreadsheet Structure

Guidelines:

A spreadsheet model is a block of occupied cells.

Cells within an *Excel* worksheet can contain either **Text** (Labels), **Numbers** (Values) or **Formulas** (calculations from number cells). **Labels** are normally used for describing the contents of the worksheet, as column or row titles for example, whereas **Values** are used for calculations.

A typical model has no blank rows or columns within it, the relationship between **Text**, **Numbers** and **Formulas** is shown below (remember this is a typical example - cell contents can be arranged in any way).

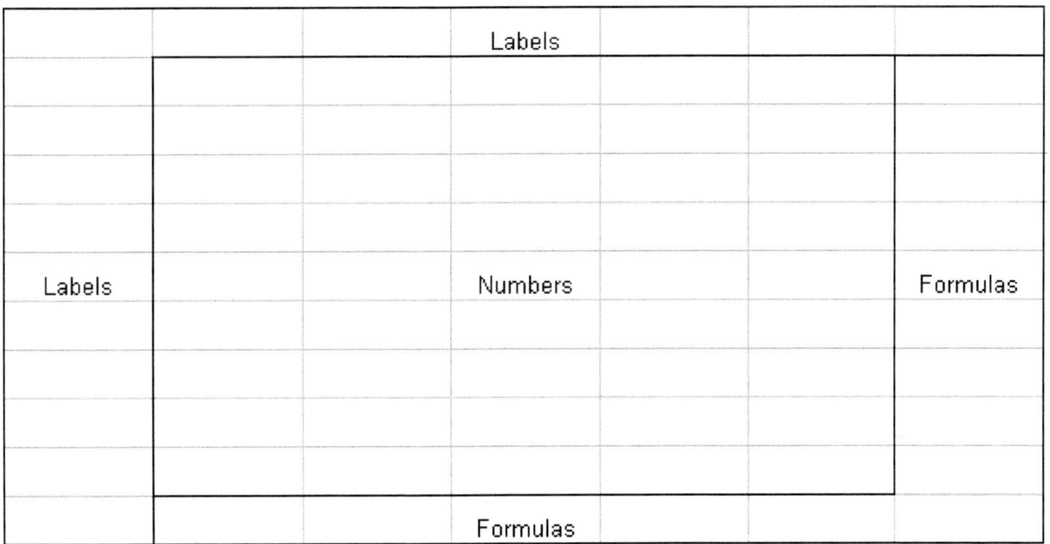

Spreadsheet shape is important when printing. Create spreadsheets so that they are either long and thin or short and fat, so that they can be paged in one direction.

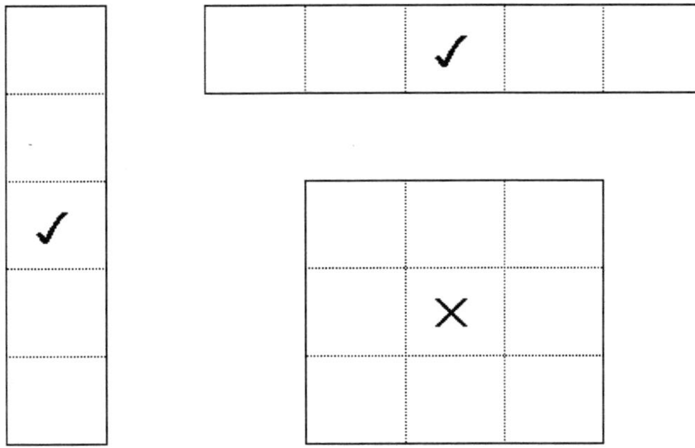

Exercise 2 - Creating a Spreadsheet

Guidelines:

Workbooks can contain many sheets. When creating a spreadsheet model, start on **Sheet1** (the default) and begin by using the top left corner. Normally a **Title** is entered in cell **A1** and the main block starts in either **A2** or **A3**.

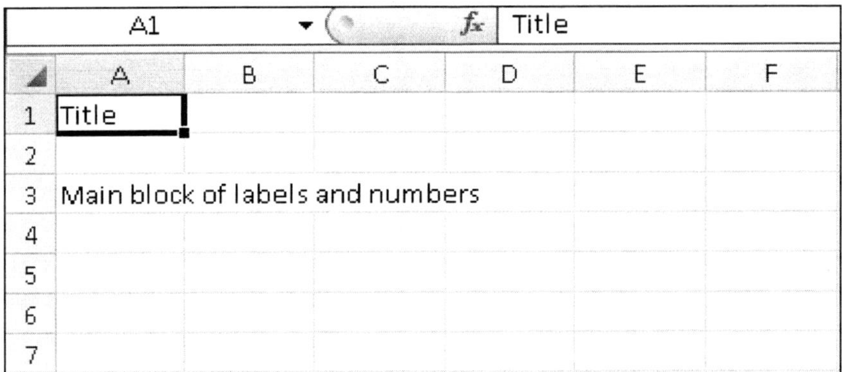

<u>Entering information into a cell</u>

To enter information into a cell, either click on the cell, or use the cursor movement (arrow) keys to place the **Active Cell** in the correct position and start typing. When entering information, the text appears in the **Formula Bar** as well as in the cell.

To complete an entry either use **<Enter>**, the cursor movement keys, click on the enter box in the **Formula Bar**, or click on another cell. When **<Enter>** is used, the active cell moves down, whereas the arrow keys allow movement in any direction, ready for the next entry.

<u>Labels</u>

Labels are entered as text and are usually placed down column **A** and across row **2** or **3** from column **B**. Text is aligned to the left by default (placed at the left edge of the cell). If the text entered does not fit completely in one cell, then the size of the text or the size of the cell can be changed (covered later in **Formatting Cells**).

<u>Numbers</u>

Select the cell, type the number and complete the entry with any of the methods described above. Numbers are right aligned (placed flush to the right edge of the cell).

Note: *To display numbers with leading zeros, start the entry with an apostrophe, e.g. '0786. The entry is now treated as text although calculations can still be performed on it without modification. Trailing zeros in decimals are displayed using formatting.*

Exercise 3 - Entering Labels

Guidelines:

Labels are normally used for describing the contents of the worksheet, as column or row titles for example.

Actions:

1. To start *Excel,* click the **Start** button and select **All Programs** and then expand the **Microsoft Office** folder. Select Microsoft Office Excel 2007 from the list.

2. Labels are entered into specific cells by typing. Cell **A1** should be active (a heavy border). If not, click on it. Type **Sandwiches Sold**. Notice that the text is displayed in the **Formula Bar** as well as in the cell.

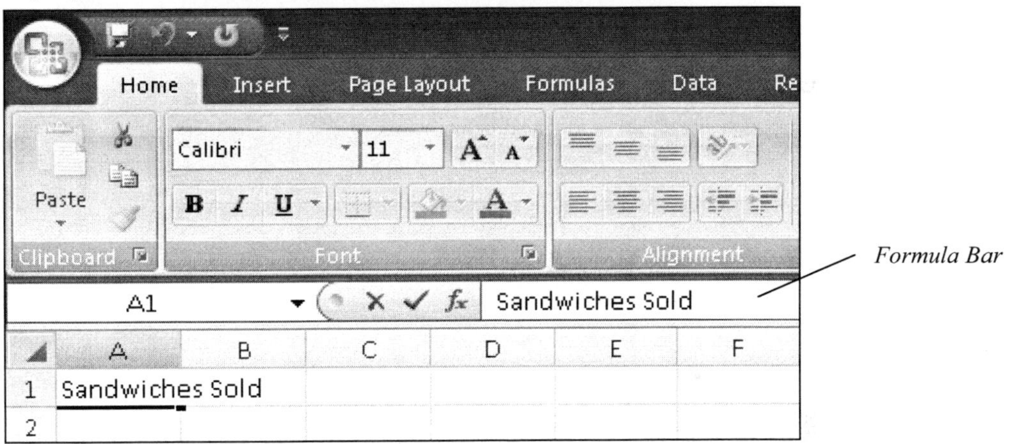

Formula Bar

3. To complete the cell entry press <**Enter**>, this causes the active cell to move down to cell **A2**. Although the text looks as though it spreads into cell **B1**, this is not the case. As cell **B1** is unused, the contents of **A1** have been displayed in full using that space.

*Note: A choice of where the active cell will be placed can be changed. Click the **Office Button,** then **Excel Options** and select **Advanced**. Any direction may be chosen under **After pressing Enter, move selection**, the default is to move to the next cell **Down**.*

4. Make cell **A3** the active cell and type **Fillings**. Enter this text by pressing <**Tab**> to move the active cell one column to the right.

5. Continue to create the spreadsheet layout by entering the labels shown below.

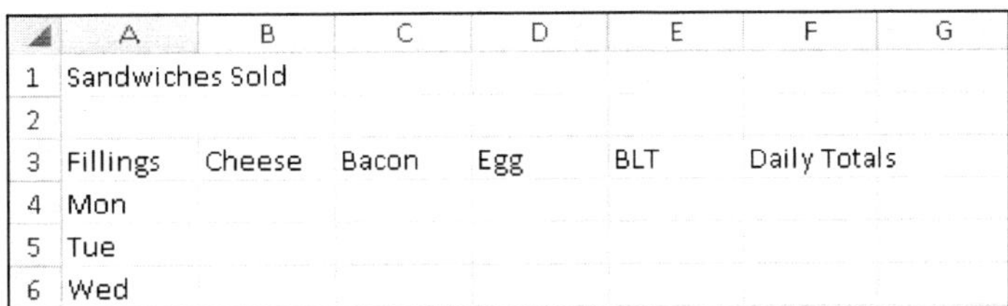

	A	B	C	D	E	F	G
1	Sandwiches Sold						
2							
3	Fillings	Cheese	Bacon	Egg	BLT	Daily Totals	
4	Mon						
5	Tue						
6	Wed						

6. Leave the workbook open, it is saved in a later exercise.

Exercise 4 - Entering Numbers

Guidelines:

Numbers must begin with one of the following characters: **0 1 2 3 4 5 6 7 8 9 . + -** or the currency symbol **£**. It is very important to enter numbers correctly. If mistakes are made, the spreadsheet will produce the wrong results.

Be careful with the use of 0 which is a numerical value and not the same as an empty cell. Zeros in cells will affect calculations using them, e.g. the functions, average and count.

Note: Using zeros for no value also detracts from the actual numbers in a worksheet. The display of zeros can, however, be prevented from being displayed. To stop zero values from being displayed, click the **Office Button** *and then* **Excel Options***, select the* **Advanced** *section and under* **Display options for this worksheet***, uncheck* **Show a zero in cells that have zero value***. Click* **OK***.*

Actions:

1.	This exercise uses the layout created in the previous exercise. If this is not available, go back and re-enter the data.

2.	Enter the extra labels in column **A**, then make cell **B4** the active cell and enter the rest of the numeric data as shown below.

	A	B	C	D	E	F	G
1	Sandwiches Sold						
2							
3	Fillings	Cheese	Bacon	Egg	BLT	Daily Totals	
4	Mon	24	30	16	29		
5	Tue	20	32	13	23		
6	Wed	21	23	20	27		
7	Thu	16	26	19	23		
8	Fri	17	34	18	33		
9	Total						
10							

3.	Do **NOT** close the workbook as it is saved in the next exercise.

Note: Remember that all values are placed automatically to the right edge of the column and the labels to the left.

Exercise 5 - Saving a New Workbook

Guidelines:

After creating worksheets, they need to be saved as a workbook so they can be used again.

The **Save** process includes selecting a location to save to and giving the workbook a name.

Actions:

1. The workbook should be open from the previous exercise, if not go back and re-create the data.

2. Click the **Office Button** and select **Save As** to display the **Save As** dialog box.

Note: When saving an unnamed workbook, click the **Office Button** and select the **Save** or **Save As** or click the **Save** button, on the **Quick Access Toolbar**. All these commands display the **Save As** dialog box.

3. The default workbook name **Book#.xlsx** (where **#** is a number) is in the **File name** box.

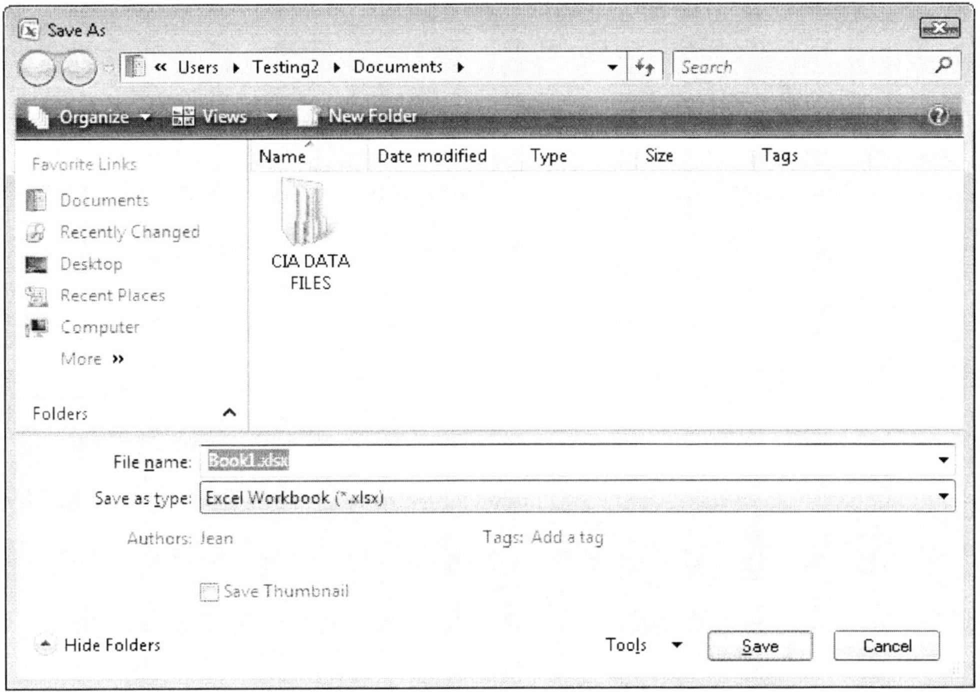

4. The default file name is already highlighted, type **Sandwiches** as the new file name to replace the default name.

continued over

Exercise 5 - Continued

5. Workbooks are saved by default to the **Documents** folder on the hard drive. To select the location where the data files are stored (see *Downloading the Data Files* on page 4). Double click **CIA DATA FILES**.

6. Double click **CLAIT Plus 2006**.

7. Double click **Unit 2 Excel 2007 Data** to display the files used with this guide.

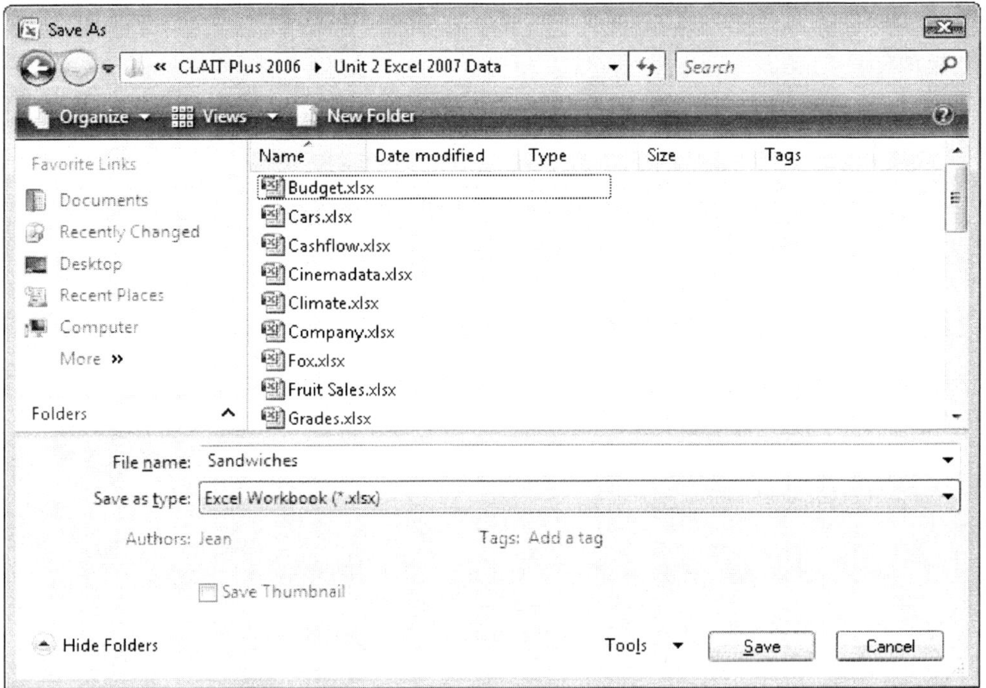

8. Change the view to **List** if necessary, using the **Views** button, **Views**. This view shows all the files in the folder.

9. Click **Save** to save the file to the correct data folder.

10. The workbook is saved as **Sandwiches** (a file extension **.xlsx** is added automatically by the program, although sometimes not displayed). The **Title Bar** changes to show the new filename, **Sandwiches**.

11. Leave the workbook open for the next exercise.

Exercise 6 - Closing a Workbook

Guidelines:

It is possible to have more than one workbook open at a time. Usually however, the current workbook is closed before opening a new one.

When closing a workbook, a warning dialog box will be displayed if any changes have been made to the workbook since it was last saved.

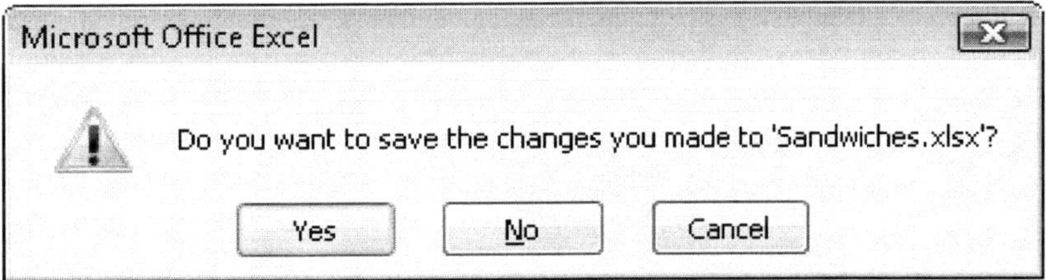

The user will be asked if they wish to save the changes and the options **Yes, No** and **Cancel** will be displayed. Selecting **Yes** will save the file under its original name before closing, **No** will close the file without saving and **Cancel** will return to the worksheet.

Actions:

1. The workbook **Sandwiches** should be open from the previous exercise, if not open it.

2. Click the **Office Button** and select **Close** to close the workbook. In this instance no changes have been made to the workbook since it was last saved, so it will close <u>without</u> displaying the **Save Changes** dialog box (if the dialog box does appear, click **No**).

Note: *The **Close Window** button,* [X] *can be used to close a workbook. Be careful not to close Excel.*

Exercise 7 - Revision

1. Start a new workbook by clicking the **Office Button** and selecting **New**. The **Blank Workbook** option is selected by default. Click the **Create** button.

*Note: Alternatively click the **Office Button, New** and double click **Blank Workbook**.*

2. Create the layout shown below, entering your own name in cell **A1**.

	A	B	C	D	E
1	Name				
2					
3	Number	First	Second	Result	
4	Add	200	50		
5	Subtract	200	50		
6	Multiply	200	50		
7	Divide	200	50		
8					

3. Save the workbook as **Calculations** to the **Unit 2 Excel 2007 Data** folder.

4. Close the **Calculations** workbook.

5. Start a new workbook.

6. Create the following worksheet:

	A	B	C	D
1	Formatting Section			
2				
3	Exercise	Title		
4		39	General Formatting	
5		40	Format Cells	
6		41	Format Number	
7		42	Date and Time	
8		43	Alignment	
9		44	Wrap Text	
10		45	Merge Cells	
11		46	Text Orientation	
12		47	Borders	
13		48	Revision	

7. Save the workbook as **Formatting Section** to the **Unit 2 Excel 2007 Data** folder.

8. Close the **Formatting Section** workbook.

Section 2

Opening and Importing

By the end of this Section you should be able to:

Open a Workbook

Import Data

Save in Different Formats

Exercise 8 - Opening a Workbook

Guidelines:

Workbooks saved to disk are only useful if they can be opened to use again.

Actions:

1. Click the **Office Button**, and select **Open**, to display the **Open** dialog box.

2. The **Unit 2 Excel 2007 Data** folder should be displayed, if not, locate it, using either the **Favorite Links** or the **Folders List** (click **Folders**).

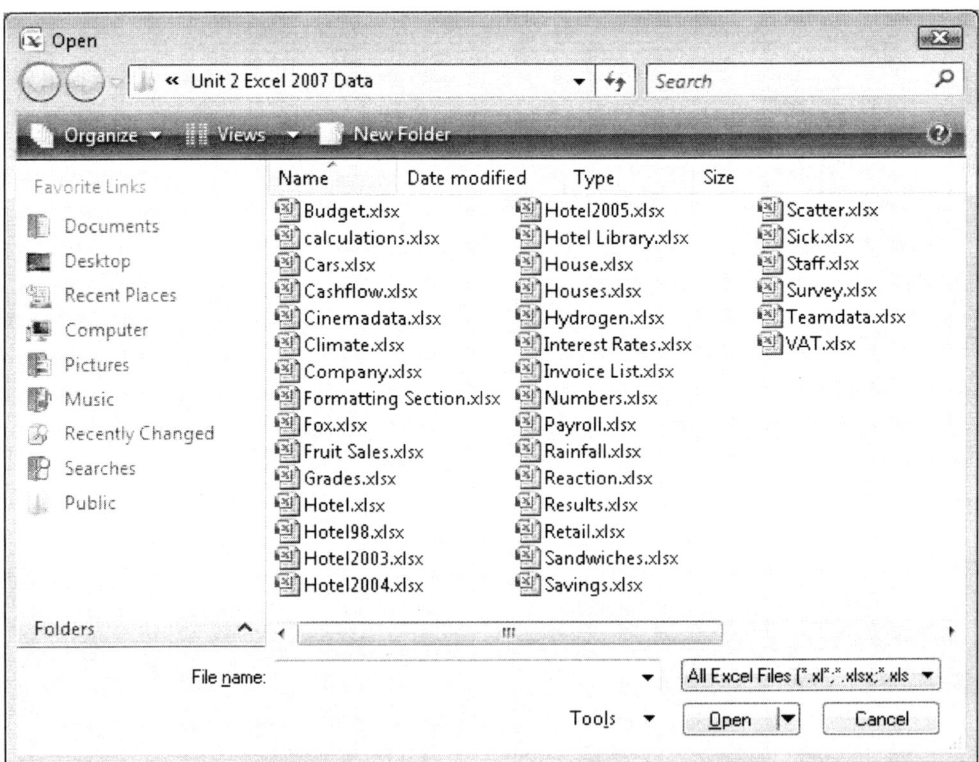

3. In the list of files, click on **Sandwiches**. This is the workbook that is to be opened. Click the **Open** button, **Open**.

Note: *Double clicking on its name in the list will also open the workbook.*

4. It should be exactly as it was when saved earlier. Close the workbook.

5. After saving files, the most recently used nine workbooks (although the number can be changed) are shown in the **Recent Documents** from the **Office Button** menu. To open a recently saved workbook, click on the **Office Button** and then click **Calculations** (this is the quickest way to open workbooks that are being continuously worked on, created in Exercise 7).

6. Close the workbook **Calculations**.

Exercise 9 - Importing Data

Guidelines:

Data can be imported into an *Excel* worksheet from a variety of external sources, including *Word* documents and *Access* databases, provided that certain criteria are met:

- The data must exist as some recognisable form of data source.

- The text data must exist as a text file (**.txt**) and the text within the file must be capable of being separated into columns by specifying recognised separators, e.g. tabs, spaces, commas.

Data is often imported in a very basic file format. This is so that it can be read by different spreadsheet applications.

Actions:

1. Open *Microsoft Word* (leaving *Excel* open) , click the **Start** button, then **All Programs**, click **Microsoft Office** to expand the folder and then click **Microsoft Office Word 2007**.

2. Open a *Word* document from the data files called **ABCD**.

3. Click the **Show/Hide** button, ¶ , on the **Home** tab in the **Paragraph** group to display the **non-printing characters**. The **Paragraph Marks** ¶, show where the <Enter> key has been pressed and the **Tabulation Marks** →, show where the <Tab> key has been pressed. The **tabs** will act as separators when the data is imported into *Excel*.

<pre>
Sales →   1ˢᵗ·Qtr→2ⁿᵈ·Qtr→3ʳᵈ·Qtr→4ᵗʰ·Qtr¶
Company·A → 45 → 53 → 60 → 55¶
Company·B → 30 → 32 → 31 → 40¶
Company·C → 51 → 49 → 34 → 39¶
Company·D → 20 → 23 → 29 → 27¶
</pre>

4. The document must be saved as a plain text file. Click the **Office Button** selecting **Save As**. Enter **Tabs** into the **File name** box and set the **Save as type** box to **Plain Text** (this adds a **txt** extension to the filename). Click the **Save** button,   Save   .

5. The **File Conversion** box appears, leave all settings as default, and click **OK**.

6. Close the document **Tabs** by clicking the **Office Button** and selecting **Close**.

7. Close *Word* by clicking the **Office Button** and selecting **Exit Word** (*Excel* should now be in view).

continued over

Exercise 9 - Continued

8.   Start a new workbook. Display the **Data** tab and select **From Text** from the **Get External Data** group to display the **Import Text File** dialog box.

9.   Ensure that the correct folder is displayed. Ensure that **Text Files** is shown to the right of the **File name** box. Select the filename **Tabs** and click the **Import** button, Import ▼.

10.   The **Text Import Wizard** opens at **Step 1 of 3**. Ensure that the **Delimited** option is selected in the **Original data type** section and that the **Start import at row** box is set at **1**. A basic preview of the layout of the data is shown in the lower part of the box.

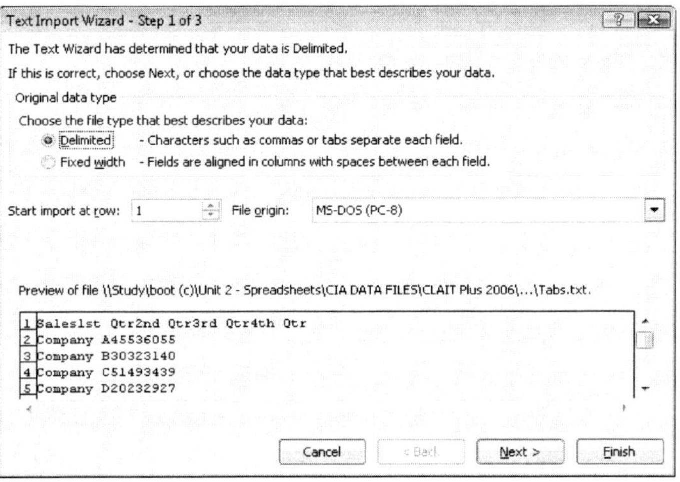

11.   Click **Next**, Next >.

12.   In **Step 2 of 3**, ensure that the **Tab** option is checked (as tabs separate the text) in the **Delimiters** section. Leave all other options boxes unchecked. A preview of the data layout is shown in the lower part of the box.

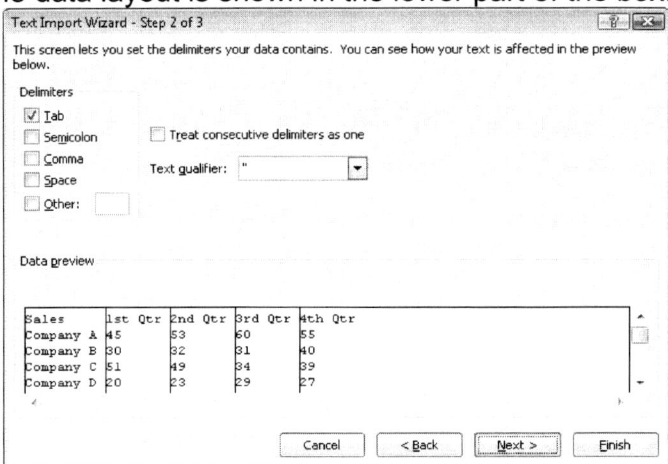

continued over

Exercise 9 - Continued

Note: *If the text being imported has quotation marks around the text, choose the appropriate marks from the **Text qualifier** box.*

13.   Click **Next**.

14.   At **Step 3 of 3** the data in any column can be formatted by selecting specific columns in the **Data preview** section and setting the required data format in the **Column data format** section. The data in all columns should be set to **General** by default. If this is not the case, correct the formats.

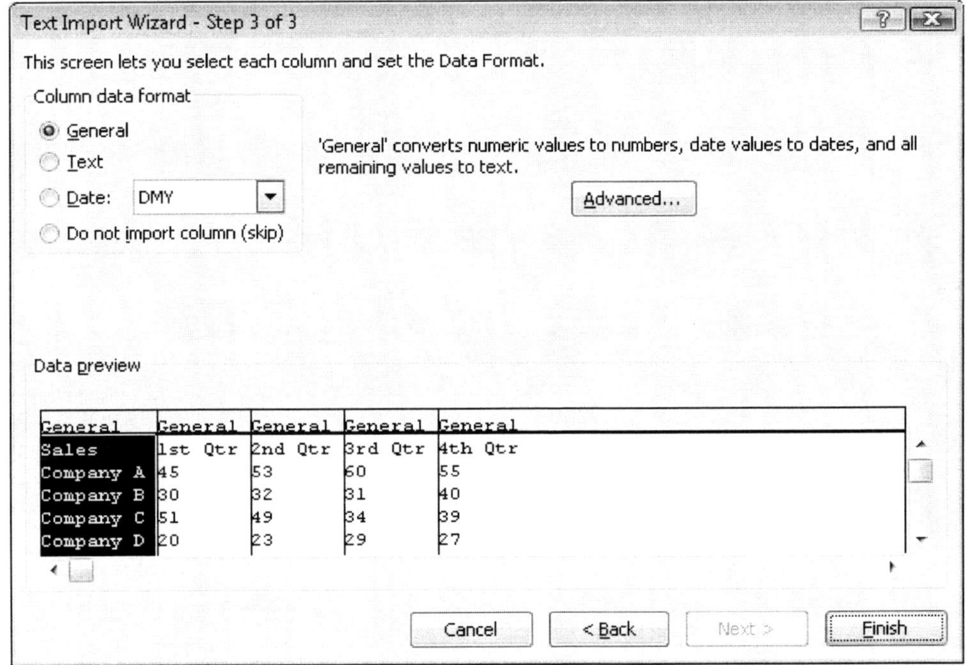

15.   Click **Finish**. The **Import Data** dialog box is displayed.

16.   Ensure that the **Existing Worksheet** option is checked. Type **C5** into the box.

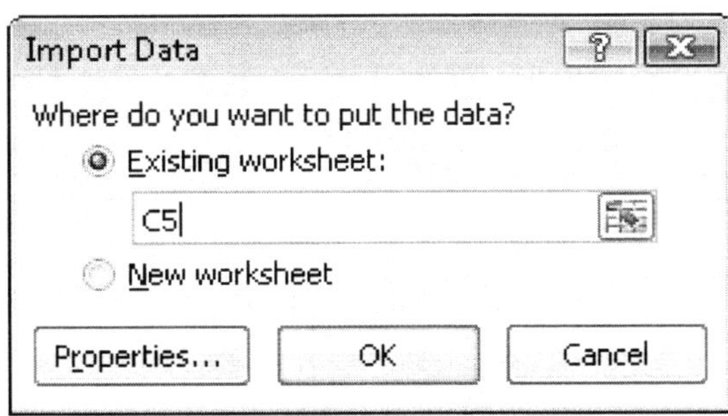

17.   Click **OK**, to import the data from the text file.

18.   Save the workbook as **Import** and then close it.

Exercise 10 - Saving in Different Formats

Guidelines:

Workbooks can be saved in a variety of formats, including older versions of *Excel* and associated products.

Actions:

1. Open the workbook **Grades**.

2. This workbook cannot be opened in any versions of *Excel* or other spreadsheet programs without being saved in the correct format. To save the workbook in a different format click the **Office Button** and select **Save As**.

3. In the **File name** box enter **Test Format**.

4. Click the drop down for the **Save as type** box. Select **Excel 97-2003 Workbook (*.xls)**.

5. Click Save.

Note: *If a workbook contains features that are not supported in the chosen format, an error message is displayed about losing formatting. Click **Yes** to save in the required format.*

6. The workbook will not look any different, but can now be opened in *Excel 97, 2000, XP or 2003*. Close the workbook.

Exercise 11 - Revision

1. Start a new workbook and import the text file **Teams.txt**.

2. Choose the **Delimiter**, which splits the data into columns (the data in this example is separated by commas and not tabs).

3. Apply the " **Text qualifier** so no quotation marks appear on the **Data preview**.

4. Place the data on the **Existing worksheet** so it appears as below.

	A	B	C	D	E	F	G	H	I	J
1	Team	Played	Won	Drawn	Lost	For	Against	Goal Diff	Points	
2	Arsenal	8	5	1	2	11	7	4	16	
3	Tottenham	7	4	1	2	13	10	3	13	
4	Liverpool	7	3	1	3	10	9	1	10	
5	Everton	8	4	1	3	14	9	5	13	
6	Leicester	8	3	2	3	11	10	1	11	
7	Southampton	7	3	0	4	10	13	-3	9	
8	Newcastle	8	1	1	6	16	19	-3	4	
9	Middlesborough	8	4	0	4	10	12	-2	12	
10	Sunderland	10	5	2	2	14	8	6	17	
11	West Ham United	6	4	1	1	9	4	5	13	
12	Chelsea	6	4	1	1	9	3	6	13	
13	Manchester United	8	6	2	0	20	7	13	20	
14	Leeds United	8	5	1	2	14	9	5	16	
15	Aston Villa	8	5	1	2	10	6	4	16	
16	Sheffield Wednesday	8	0	1	7	3	23	-20	1	
17	Watford	8	3	0	5	5	8	-3	9	
18	Derby County	8	2	2	4	7	14	-7	8	
19	Wimbledon	8	1	4	3	12	17	-5	7	
20	Coventry	8	1	2	5	10	13	-3	5	
21	Bradford City	7	1	2	4	3	9	-6	5	

5. Save the workbook as **League**.

6. Close the workbook.

7. Open the workbook **League**.

8. The workbook needs to be converted to be able to be used in *other spreadsheet packages*. Save the workbook as **League4** in a **CSV (Comma delimited)** file format.

9. At the prompt to lose multiple sheets click **OK** and **Yes** to the loss of formatting message.

10. Close the workbook <u>without</u> saving the changes.

Section 3

Formulas

By the end of this Section you should be able to:

Create Simple Formulas

Understand Mathematical Operators

Use Brackets

Calculate Percentages

Select Cells with the Mouse to Create Formulas

Understand Ranges

Use AutoSum

Copy and Paste Formulas

Use the Fill Handle

Check Formulas for Errors

Exercise 12 - Introducing Formulas

Guidelines:

A calculation in *Excel* is called a **Formula**. Formulas are used to calculate answers from numbers entered on the sheet, e.g. add a column of numbers, total sales for the year, calculate net profit in a month, etc. Formulas automatically calculate results from the data. The original data can be changed, but the formula will automatically recalculate. This allows results to be projected from different data, but using the same formula. All formulas begin with an equals sign (=), followed by the calculation. Cell references are used in formulas in *Excel*.

Actions:

1. Open the workbook **Calculations** that was created in Exercise 7. If you have not completed Exercise 7, create the layout shown below, placing your own name in cell **A1** and leaving cell **D4** empty for the moment.

2. The contents of cells **B4** and **C4** are to be added together. Click on cell **D4** to make it the active cell. Type **=b4+c4**, without leaving spaces (the **+** symbol on the numeric keypad at the right of the keyboard may be used for the add sign). Ignore any menus that may appear.

Note: To use the numeric keypad for number entries, the **Num Lock** light must be on. If it is not on, press the **<Num Lock>** key. When entering cell references, like **B4**, it does not matter if they are entered in capitals or not, as Excel converts them to uppercase.

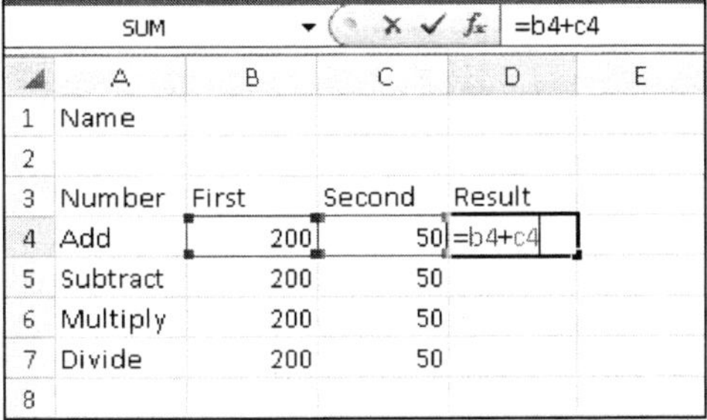

3. Complete the formula in **D4** by pressing **<Enter>**.

4. Click back on cell **D4** and notice that the answer to the calculation, **250**, is displayed in the cell, while the actual cell contents **=B4+C4** are displayed on the **Formula Bar**.

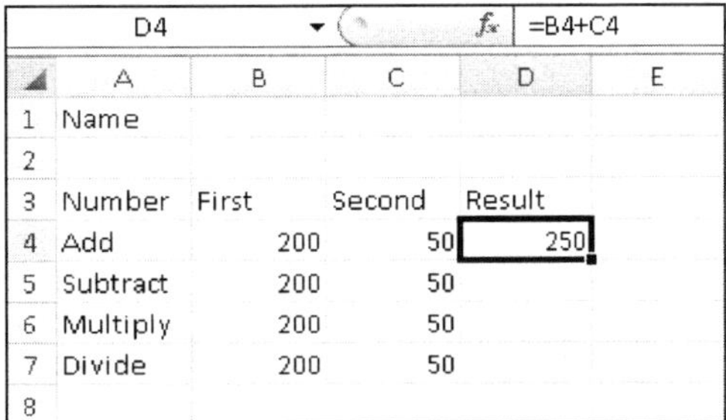

5. Save the workbook as **Calculations2** and leave it open.

Exercise 13 - Mathematical Operators

Guidelines:

The basic mathematical operators are add, subtract, multiply and divide. The symbols on a keyboard are slightly different to those used normally and are:

    +   Add

    -   Subtract

    __*__   **Multiply**

    /   Divide

These symbols appear twice on the keyboard, one set placed around the main keyboard and the other set on the numeric keypad (right side). The numeric keypad is easier to use because the keys are closer together and the **<Shift>** key is not needed.

Other mathematical operations are used via **Functions**, covered in a later Section. *Office 2007* has a **Function Library** group on the **Formulas** tab which contains the most used functions.

Actions:

1. The workbook **Calculations2** should still be open from the previous exercise. If not, open it.

2. The number in cell **C5** is to be subtracted from the number in cell **B5**. Make cell **D5** the active cell and enter the formula **=b5-c5**. Complete the entry by pressing **<Enter>**. Cell **D5** should display the answer **150**.

3. Cell **D6** will be used to multiply together the contents of cells **B6** and **C6**. Enter the formula **=b6*c6** into cell **D6**. The answer should be **10000**.

4. Cell **D7** will be used to divide the contents of cell **B7** by the contents of cell **C7**. Make cell **D7** the active cell and enter the formula **=b7/c7**. Cell **D7** should display the answer **4**.

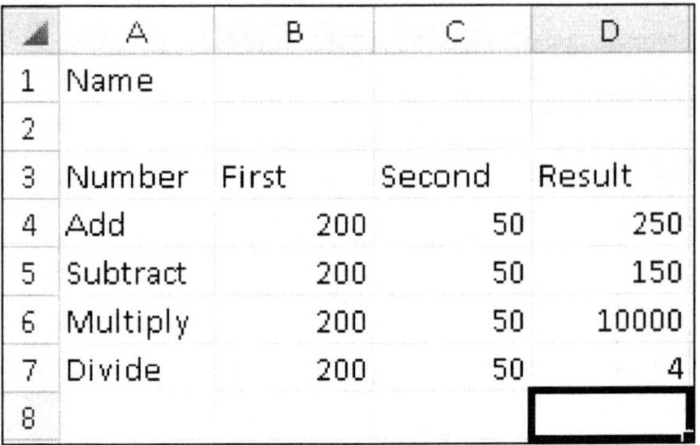

	A	B	C	D
1	Name			
2				
3	Number	First	Second	Result
4	Add	200	50	250
5	Subtract	200	50	150
6	Multiply	200	50	10000
7	Divide	200	50	4
8				

5. Save the workbook and close it.

Exercise 14 - Brackets

Guidelines:

When more than one operator is used in a single formula, then the order becomes important, e.g. **D23+E17/E19**. *Excel* performs calculations in this order: **B**rackets over **D**ivision, **M**ultiplication, **A**ddition and finally **S**ubtraction (the **BODMAS** theory). So in this example **E17** would be divided by **E19** then added to **D23**. Brackets are added to force *Excel* to perform calculations in a different order.

Actions:

1. Start a new blank workbook and create the spreadsheet layout shown below.

	A	B	C
1	Profit		
2			
3		Product 1	
4	Sold at	15	
5	Bought at	10	
6	Number	20	
7	Profit		
8			

2. The profit per unit is calculated by subtracting the **Bought at** price from the **Sold at** price. The overall profit per product may then be calculated by multiplying the profit per item by the number of units sold. Make cell **B7** the active cell and enter the formula **=b4-b5*b6**.

3. Press **<Enter>** and the answer is displayed as **-185**, a loss! This is because *Excel* follows the BODMAS theory and carries out the multiplication (**10*20=200**) before the subtraction (**15-200=negative 185**).

4. To correct the situation delete the contents of cell **B7** and re-enter the formula as **=(b4-b5)*b6 <Enter>**.

5. Notice how the brackets ensure that the subtraction (**15-10**) is carried out first and then the multiplication (**5*20**), so that the correct answer of **100** is displayed.

6. Save the workbook as **Brackets** and leave it open.

continued over

Exercise 14 - Continued

7. Click the **Sheet2** tab. Enter the following data, starting at cell **B2**.

	A	B	C	D
1				
2		Price (p)	Number	
3		20	2	
4		30	5	
5				
6		Total (£)		
7				

8. In cell **C6**, the total income will be calculated by multiplying the **Price** by **Number** e.g. **20** by **2** and **30** by **5** and then adding these together, then dividing by **100** to give the price in **pounds**. Enter the formula **=B3*C3+B4*C4/100**.

C6			f_x	=B3*C3+B4*C4/100	

	A	B	C	D	E	F
1						
2		Price (p)	Number			
3		20	2			
4		30	5			
5						
6		Total (£)	41.5			
7						

9. The answer is **£41.50**, which is not correct. Brackets must be used to make sure *Excel* performs the calculations in the right order, e.g. the multiplications first, the addition second and the division last.

10. Click on cell **C6** and press the **<Delete>** key.

11. Now enter the correct formula, **=((B3*C3)+(B4*C4))/100** (Brackets are always used in matching pairs).

C6			f_x	=((B3*C3)+(B4*C4))/100	

	A	B	C	D	E	F
1						
2		Price (p)	Number			
3		20	2			
4		30	5			
5						
6		Total (£)	1.9			
7						

Note: *When brackets appear inside other brackets, the inside brackets are always calculated first. In the example, the two multiplications are calculated first, then added together and finally the division is performed.*

12. Save the workbook and leave it open for the next exercise.

Exercise 15 - Selecting Cells with the Mouse

Guidelines:

When entering formulas that involve the use of cell references, e.g. **=E6+F6** or even **=GZ1207+GZ1208** typing errors can be made. The mouse can be used to enter the cell references. This is also called **Pointing**. The mouse pointer is moved to the required cell and clicked.

Actions:

1. The workbook **Brackets** should still be open from the previous exercise. If not, open it. Click the **Sheet1** tab.

2. Make cell **C3** active and enter the label **Product 2**.

3. In cell **C4** enter a **Sold at** price of **20**.

4. In cell **C5** enter a **Bought at** price of **10**.

5. In cell **C6** enter the **Number** value of **15**

6. Make cell **C7** active and begin a formula by typing **=(** then instead of typing the cell reference, click on cell **C4** to enter the reference into the formula.

	A	B	C	D
1	Profit			
2				
3		Product 1	Product 2	
4	Sold at	15	20	
5	Bought at	10	10	
6	Number	20	15	
7	Profit	100	=(C4	
8				

7. Use the keyboard to enter a **-** sign and then click on cell **C5**. Type **)*** and then click on cell **C6**. Press **<Enter>** to complete the formula and confirm that **C7** displays the correct result of **150**.

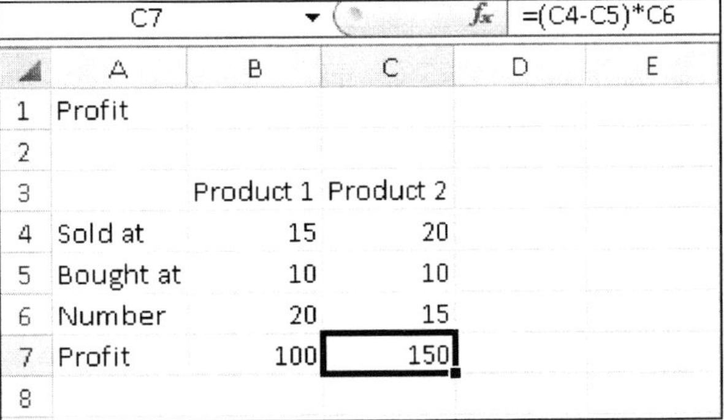

C7				f_x	=(C4-C5)*C6

	A	B	C	D	E
1	Profit				
2					
3		Product 1	Product 2		
4	Sold at	15	20		
5	Bought at	10	10		
6	Number	20	15		
7	Profit	100	150		
8					

*The **Formula Bar** shows the formula and the cell the answer*

8. Save the workbook and close it.

Exercise 16 - Percentages

Guidelines:

Percentages are displayed with a percentage symbol, e.g. 25%. A percentage is a fraction or decimal displayed differently. Percent means per hundred. 20% is 20/100 as a fraction or 0.2 as a decimal.

There is a **Percent Style** button, 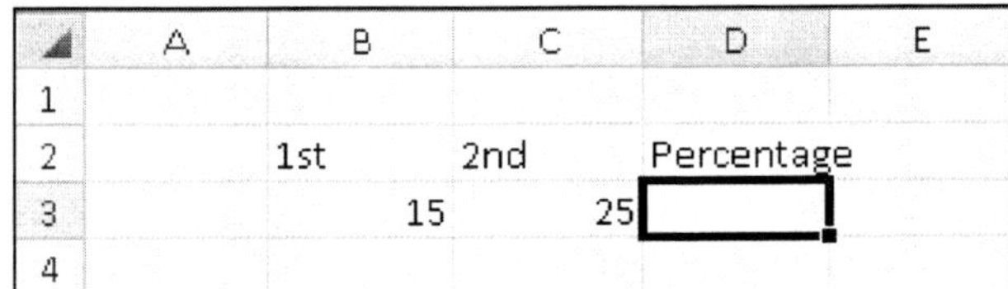, that changes a decimal to a percentage.

Actions:

1. Start a new workbook and create the following worksheet.

◢	A	B	C	D	E
1					
2		1st	2nd	Percentage	
3		15	25		
4					

2. To display the first number as a percentage of the second in **D3**, enter the formula **=B3/C3** using any method.

3. To format the answer as a percentage, click the **Percent Style** button, 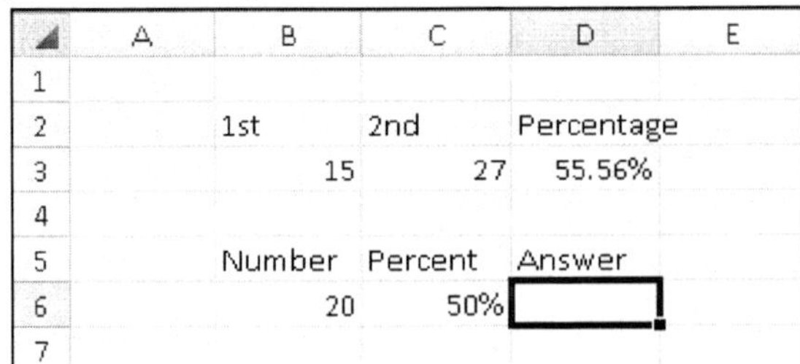 from the **Number** group on the **Home** tab.

4. Change the second number to **27** and press <Enter>, notice that the percentage value changes automatically.

5. To display percentage with two decimal places, make the active cell **D3** and click in the **Format Number** box drop down, in the **Number** group and select **Percentage** to display the cell as **55.56%**.

6. Add the following data starting at cell **B5**.

◢	A	B	C	D	E
1					
2		1st	2nd	Percentage	
3		15	27	55.56%	
4					
5		Number	Percent	Answer	
6		20	50%		
7					

Note: To enter **50%** in cell **C6**, type **50** followed by the percent key <**Shift 5**>, or enter **0.5** and use the **Percent Style** button.

7. To find 50 percent of 20, in cell **D6** enter the formula **=B6*C6**. The answer is **10** (half of 20 is 10).

8. Enter **86** in **B6** and **45%** in **C6**. Press <Enter> to display the answer, **38.7**.

9. Close the workbook <u>without</u> saving.

Exercise 17 - Ranges

Guidelines:

A **Range** is a rectangular collection of cells. Just as single cells are identified by a cell reference, ranges are identified by the cells of their outer limits, e.g. the four cells **B2, B3, C2** and **C3** is the range **B2:C3**.

Ranges are selected by pressing the mouse button and holding it down, then dragging to highlight a range of cells (called **click and drag**). Entire rows or columns can be selected by clicking the row or column headings. By clicking and dragging the row or column headings, groups of rows or columns can be selected.

Actions:

1. On a new worksheet, point and click on cell **B2** and with the mouse button held down, drag down and to the right so that a range of four cells is highlighted, as shown below.

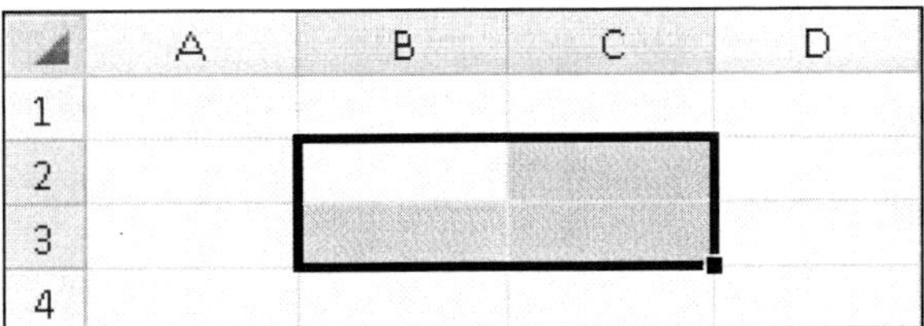

2. Release the mouse button. Notice that the first cell in the range contains the cell reference (is white) and the other cells are highlighted in pale blue.

3. Click anywhere on the worksheet to remove the selected range.

4. More than one range can be selected by pressing <**Ctrl**> whilst clicking and dragging. Select the range **B2:C3** again. Press and hold down the <**Ctrl**> key. Click and drag the range **C5:D6**. Release the <**Ctrl**> key. There should now be two separate ranges highlighted.

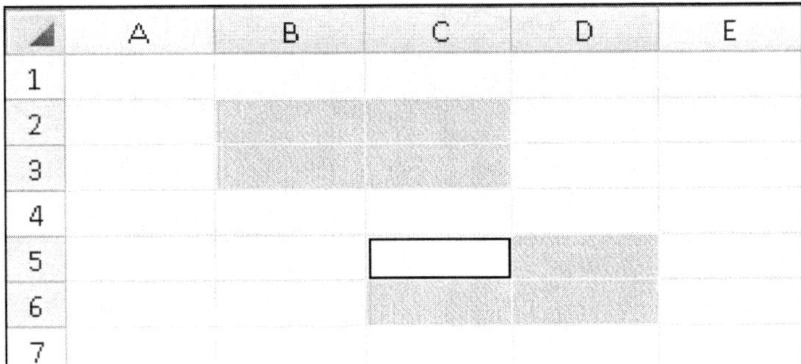

5. Click anywhere on the worksheet to remove the selected ranges.

6. Click on the **B** in the column heading. Column **B** is now highlighted. Click anywhere to deselect it.

continued over

Exercise 17 - Continued

7.   Click and drag in the row heading, from **5** to **7**. The three rows are selected. Click anywhere on the worksheet to remove the selection.

8.   When selecting a range the mouse control has to be very precise. Sometimes the range is not exactly the right one, it may be 1 row or column short. Click and drag the range **C3:G7**.

9.   The range can be extended by holding down the <**Shift**> key and clicking on a cell to extend the range. Hold <**Shift**> and click on cell **G9**. The range is extended.

10.   Click anywhere on the worksheet to remove the selection.

11.   A range can be selected without dragging using the above method. Click on cell **B2**, hold <**Shift**> and click on cell **G12**, to select the range **B2:G12**.

Note: *If the range is larger than the screen, stay in the grey areas next to the worksheet if dragging, as the selection process is very fast if the pointer touches the edge of the screen.*

12.   Select the range **C5:Z5** by dragging. Deselect the range.

13.   Select the same range **C5:Z5** by clicking in cell **C5**, scrolling across to column **Z**, holding <**Shift**> and clicking in cell **Z5**.

14.   Close the workbook <u>without</u> saving.

Exercise 18 - AutoSum

Guidelines:

The most common formula is addition. This calculation has been simplified by the creation of a **Function** called **Sum**. Functions (covered in full in a later Section) are pre-created formulas. There are buttons on the **Ribbon** called **AutoSum** that creates the **Sum** function automatically.

Actions:

1. Open the workbook **Sandwiches**. This should have been created earlier, if not, go back to Exercise 4 and re-create the spreadsheet layout.

2. Click on cell **F4**. A formula needs to be entered here that will add up the contents of the four cells **B4**, **C4**, **D4** and **E4**. Using the mouse to select each of the cells, enter the formula **=B4+C4+D4+E4**.

3. This method of adding cell contents soon becomes unusable, as more numbers need to be added. To avoid the creation of long and unwieldy formulas, a function: **SUM** is available within *Excel* to add together the contents of a group of cells. A button is provided on the toolbar to perform this function automatically. Make cell **B9** the active cell.

4. Display the **Formulas** tab and click the **AutoSum** button, ∑ AutoSum in the **Function Library** group.

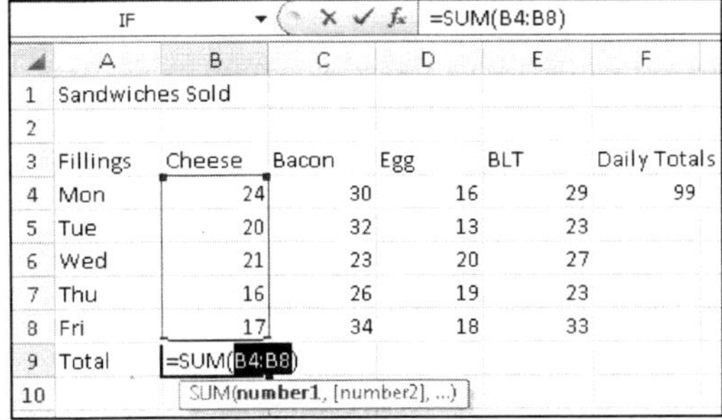

Note: *There is also an **AutoSum** button on the **Home** tab in the **Editing** group,* ∑.

5. **AutoSum** scans vertically upwards, searching for cells containing numbers. It identifies the numbers in cells **B4** to **B8** and uses those cell references to create the function **=SUM(B4:B8)**. Since this is the correct calculation, press <**Enter**> to accept the function and display **98**.

6. Make cell **F4** active and click ∑ AutoSum to replace the existing formula. This time **AutoSum** scans vertically upwards but there are no numbers above so it scans left and identifies the range of cells from **B4** to **E4** inclusive. Press <**Enter**> to complete the function. The answer should be **99**, the same as displayed by the original formula.

Note: ***AutoSum** only works without any help when numbers have already been entered into the worksheet. If **AutoSum** has numbers in both directions it will sum upwards by default.*

7. The other totals will be added in a later exercise. Save the workbook as **Sandwiches2** and close it.

Exercise 19 - Copy and Paste

Guidelines:

Rather than repeatedly typing the same data into several cells, the data can be copied and then pasted.

The **Copy** command can be used to copy labels, values and formulas. The selected cells are placed in an area of *Windows* called the **Clipboard**, from where they can then be **Pasted** back into other locations.

Actions:

1. Start a new workbook.

2. Make the cell **B3** active and type **HELLO <Enter>**.

3. To copy this cell, click on cell **B3** and then click the **Copy** button, from the **Clipboard** group on the **Home** tab.

Note: *An alternative method is to press <**Ctrl C**>.*

4. The selected cell will now have a broken border (called a **Marquee**) and the message **Select destination and press ENTER or choose Paste** is displayed in the **Status Bar**.

5. Click on cell **B7** and press **<Enter>**. The contents of **B3** will now be pasted into **B7**. The contents of **B3** remain unchanged. Note that **B3** no longer has a broken border.

6. Enter **65** into cell **C6**, select the cell and click the **Copy** button, .

7. Move to **B9** and click the **Paste** button, . Note that **C6** still has a broken border, indicating that its contents can be pasted again if required.

Note: *A **Paste Options Smart Tag**, , will be displayed next to the pasted range. Clicking on this tag would display a selection of options concerning the paste process. These are not covered in this guide.*

Note: *An alternative method is to press <**Ctrl V**>.*

8. Move to **B10** and paste again.

9. Press **<Esc>** to end the pasting and remove the marquee around **C6**.

10. Close the workbook <u>without</u> saving the changes.

Exercise 20 - Using the Fill Handle

Guidelines:

Ranges can be quickly filled with data by using the **Fill Handle**, which appears when the cursor is placed over the bottom right corner of the active cell. Cell contents can either be copied or used as the basis for a numeric series.

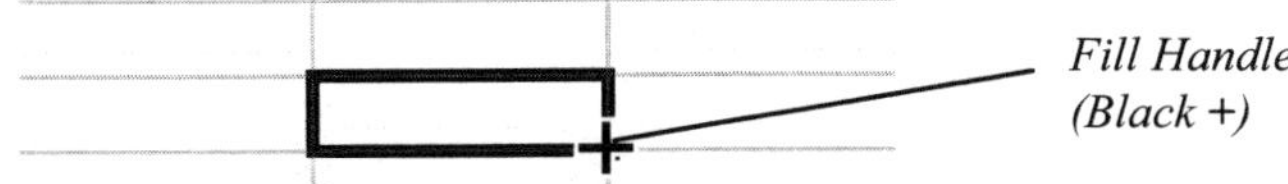

It is only possible to drag in one direction, i.e. along a row <u>or</u> down a column.

An extra feature of dragging the **Fill Handle** is the ability to automatically fill ranges with series such as months of the year, days of the week and dates.

Actions:

1. Open the workbook **Sandwiches2**.

2. Click on the **Sheet2** tab to view a blank sheet within **Sandwiches2**.

3. Type your first name into cell **B2**. Complete the entry.

4. Select **B2** again and move the mouse pointer to the **Fill Handle** of **B2**. Click and drag the cell along to **G2**.

5. In **E4** enter **63**. Click and drag the **Fill Handle** of **E4** across to **I4**. The entry **63** is repeated.

6. Click the cell **E4** again. Hold <**Ctrl**> while dragging the **Fill Handle** to cell **E9**.

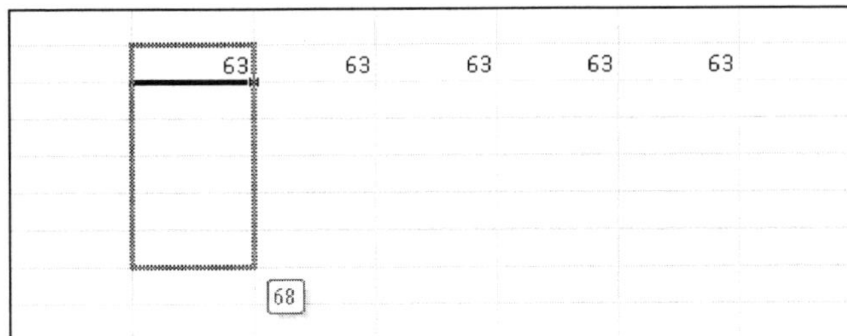

7. Release the mouse button to fill the cells with increasing numbers. This method is very useful for quickly numbering cells, especially rows.

8. In **A10** enter **January**. Click and drag the fill handle of **A10** along to **H10**.

9. In **A13** enter **1st**.

10. Click and drag the fill handle of **A13** down to **A22**. This is very useful when creating calendars.

continued over

Exercise 20 - Continued

11.   Click the **Sheet1** tab to display the sandwich sales data.

12.   Formulas can also be copied using the **Fill Handle**. The formulas in cells **B9** and **F4** can be copied in this way to save re-typing.

13.   With the active cell as **B9**, drag the **Fill Handle** across to **F9**.

	A	B	C	D	E	F	G
1	Sandwiches Sold						
2							
3	Fillings	Cheese	Bacon	Egg	BLT	Daily Totals	
4	Mon	24	30	16	29	99	
5	Tue	20	32	13	23		
6	Wed	21	23	20	27		
7	Thur	16	26	19	23		
8	Fri	17	34	18	33		
9	Total	98	145	86	135	99	
10							
11							

Note: *E9 will show the sum of column E and F9 will show the sum of column F although column F is incomplete at the moment.*

Note: *The **AutoFill Options Smart Tag**, appears. This allows different formatting to be selected. Performing any other unrelated action removes it.*

14.   Click in cell **E9** and check the **Formula Bar** to see that the formula has been updated automatically to sum column **E** instead of column **B**.

15.   To complete column **F** make the active cell **F4** and drag the fill handle down to **F8**. The completed spreadsheet should look the same as below.

	A	B	C	D	E	F	G
1	Sandwiches Sold						
2							
3	Fillings	Cheese	Bacon	Egg	BLT	Daily Totals	
4	Mon	24	30	16	29	99	
5	Tue	20	32	13	23	88	
6	Wed	21	23	20	27	91	
7	Thu	16	26	19	23	84	
8	Fri	17	34	18	33	102	
9	Total	98	145	86	135	464	
10							

16.   Save the workbook using the same file name.

17.   Leave the workbook open for the next exercise.

Exercise 21 - Checking Formulas

Guidelines:

Spreadsheets are of little use if the formulas within them contain errors. All formulas should be checked to make sure that they are accurate.

Actions:

1. The workbook **Sandwiches2** should still be open from the previous exercise. If not, open it.

2. To check the formula in cell **F4**, click on the cell and check the formula in the **Formula Bar**, it should be **=SUM(B4:E4)**.

3. A much better way to check a formula is to double click on the required cell. Double click on cell **F4**. The formula is displayed in the cell with colour coding to show which cells are used.

4. After checking, press <**Enter**> or <**Esc**> to finish the editing.

5. Double click on cell **F9**. The range is shown in blue. Click and drag the blue range border down to start at row **12**, which moves the range being calculated in **F9**.

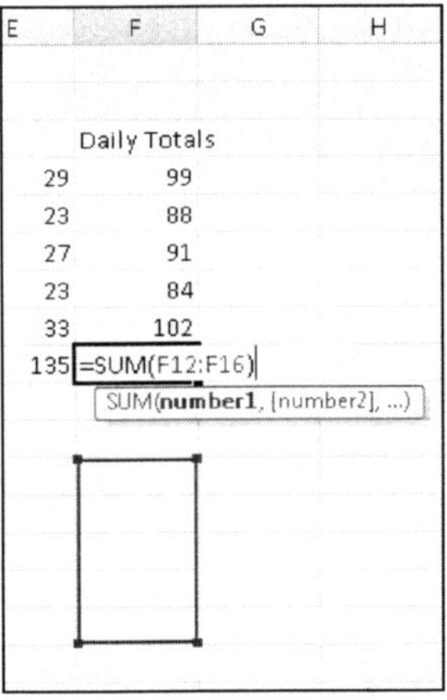

Note: *As well as moving the range it can be adjusted by moving the mouse pointer over one of the corner arrows and clicking and dragging the border.*

6. Click and drag the border up two cells, using the right corner, so the range only includes three cells.   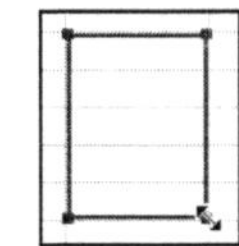

7. Move the range back to the correct position starting on row **4** (it will be two rows short). Press <**Enter**> to complete the formula.

8. Double click on cell **F9** and adjust the range to include **F7** and **F8** as before.

9. Save the changes using the same name and close **Sandwiches2**.

Exercise 22 - Revision

1. Start a new workbook.

2. The illustration below shows the number of high-tech components produced in a week by the different plants of a precision engineering company. Create the following worksheet.

	A	B	C	D	E	F
1	Week ending: 9th January 2007					
2						
3						
4	Production	Northern	Southern	Eastern	Western	Total
5	Wottnots	25078	23512	25385	24765	
6	Thingmies	16362	16391	17425	16987	
7	Widgets	11234	10959	12001	11678	
8	Doodahs	8950	9006	7123	9218	
9	Total					

3. In cell **F5**, use **AutoSum** to work out the total number of **Wottnotts** produced across the four plants.

4. In cell **B9**, calculate the total output of the **Northern** plant for the week.

5. Use the **Fill Handle** to replicate the formula in **F5** down to **F8**.

6. Copy the formula in **B9** across to **F9**.

7. What was the total production of the **Southern** plant in that week?

8. How many **Doodahs** did the four plants produce between them during the week?

9. What was the total output for all four plants?

10. Save the workbook as **Engineering**.

11. Close the workbook.

Note: *The answers for this exercise are listed in the **Answer Section** at the end of the guide.*

Section 4

Editing Cells

By the end of this Section you should be able to:

Edit Cells by Overtyping

Delete Cell Contents

Use Undo and Redo

Edit Data

Exercise 23 - Overtyping

Guidelines:

If the cell entry is short, then the simplest way to edit is to click on the cell and enter the new data. This overwrites the previous entry.

Actions:

1. Start a new workbook.

2. Type **January** into cell **A2** and press **<Enter>**.

3. Make cell **A2** the active cell and type **February**. Press <Enter> to replace **January** with **February**. The contents of any cell may be overwritten in this way.

4. Select cell **C3**. Type **2007** but <u>DON'T</u> press <Enter>, instead press **<Esc>**, the **Escape** key. This action cancels the new input and leaves the original cell content unchanged, in this case the cell is blank.

5. With **C3** still active, re-enter **2007** and once again <u>DON'T</u> press <Enter>. This time click the **Cancel** button in order to cancel the new input.

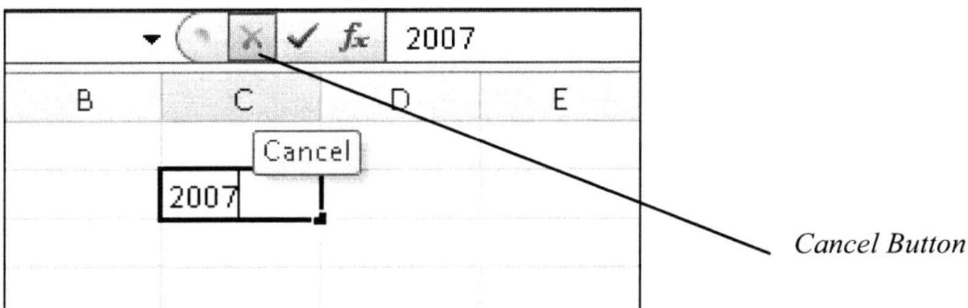

6. Close the workbook <u>without</u> saving.

7. Open the workbook **Sandwiches2**.

8. Cell **D5** should currently contain the value **13**. Click on this cell and overtype the current value with the number **25** then press <Enter>. The formulas in cells **F5** and **F9** will immediately recalculate using the new value and display the current results. (**100** and **476**)

9. Experiment by changing the values in any of the cells in the range **B4** to **E8**. Be careful not to overwrite any of the formulas in row **9** or column **F**.

10. Close the workbook <u>without</u> saving.

Exercise 24 - Deleting Cell Contents

Guidelines:

Cell contents are erased by using the keyboard or the **Clear** button, 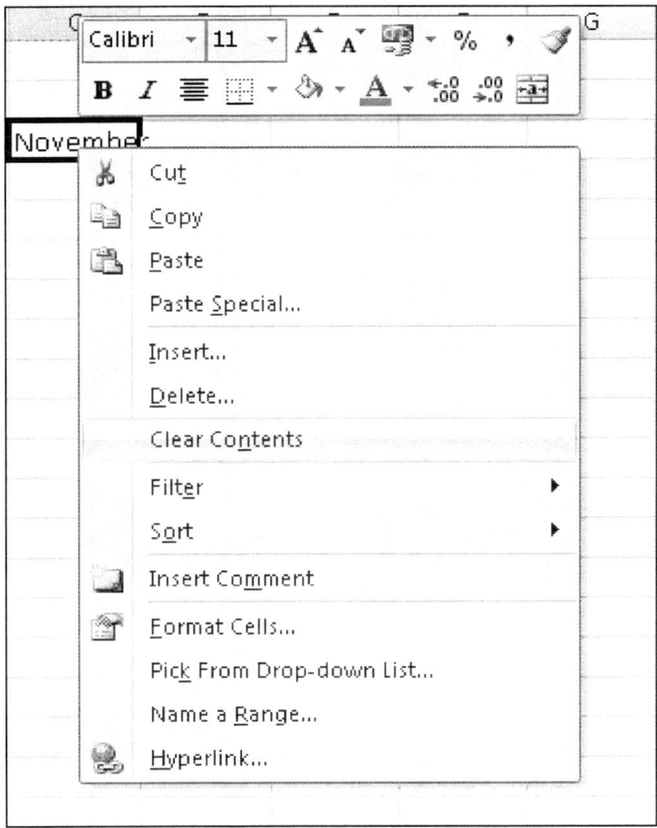 on the **Ribbon** or by right clicking and using **Clear Contents** from the shortcut menu.

Actions:

1. Open a blank workbook. Type **1952** into cell **C2** and press **<Enter>**.

2. Erase the contents of cell **C2** by clicking on it and pressing **<Delete>**.

3. In cell **B3** enter **24th** and in cell **C3** enter **November**.

4. Make cell **B3** active and click the **Clear** button, in the **Editing** group on the **Home** tab. Select **Clear Contents** from the menu.

5. Make cell **C3** active and right click on the cell selecting **Clear Contents**.

6. The worksheet should now be completely blank again. Any of the above 3 methods can be used, but using the **<Delete>** key press is the easiest.

7. Leave the workbook open for the next exercise.

Exercise 25 - Undo and Redo

Guidelines:

When editing a worksheet, the last change made can be **Undone** by using the **Undo** command. After undoing an action it can be **Redone** by using the **Redo** command.

Actions:

1. A blank workbook is open from the previous exercise. In cell **B3**, type your name then **<Enter>**.

2. Place the cursor over the **Undo** button, (the button is located on the **Quick Access Toolbar** next to the **Office** button. The **Tooltip** states **Undo Typing "name" in B3 (Ctrl+Z)**. Click the **Undo** button to remove your name from the cell.

3. The **Repeat** button, next to **Undo** changes to **Redo** after **Undo** has been used. Place the cursor over the **Redo** button, , the **Tooltip** reads, **Redo Typing "name" in B3 (Ctrl+Y)**. Click **Redo** button to restore the cell entry.

Note: *The exact wording after **Undo** and **Redo** is dependent on the action that has just been carried out.*

4. In **B3** overtype your name with **Fred <Enter>**. Click the **Undo** button, , to replace **Fred** with your name again. Click on the **Redo** button, , to restore the entry to **Fred**.

5. In cell **D6** enter **36** and in cell **F8** enter **48**.

6. Click on **D6** and delete the cell contents. Delete the contents of cell **F8**.

Note: *The **Undo**, , or **Redo**, , buttons have a history. If the associated arrow is clicked, then a list of the actions that can be **Undone** or **Redone** appears. To select more than one action, click on the lowest item in the list. Multiple actions can be undone by clicking the **Undo** button as many times as necessary.*

7. Click the **Undo** down arrow, , to display the **Undo** history.

8. Position the mouse pointer over the second clear in the list as shown in the diagram and click the mouse button to undo the last two items.

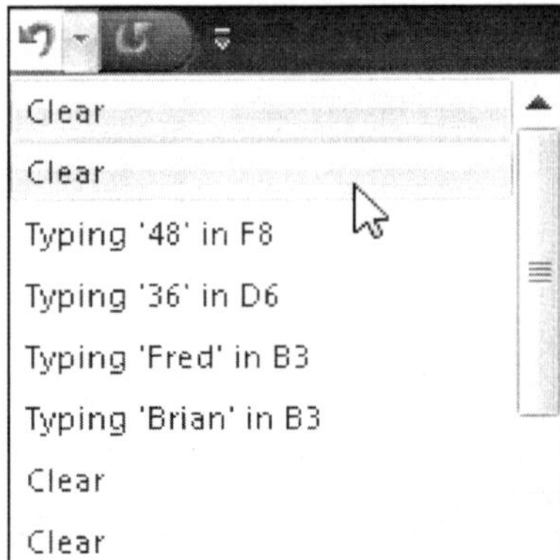

9. Close the workbook <u>without</u> saving.

Exercise 26 - Editing Data in the Formula Bar

Guidelines:

When a cell entry is long or complicated and only small changes are to be made, the changes are either made in the **Formula Bar** or in the cell itself (covered in the next exercise).

The following keys may then be used to move around and change the cell contents:

<Insert>	Insert key: Used to toggle (change) between **Insert** and **Overwrite**. When **Insert** is selected, the existing text moves to the right as new text is typed. When **Insert** is not selected the new information simply overwrites the old
<Delete>	Delete key: Removes the character following the cursor
<Backspace>	Backspace key: Erases the character immediately preceding the current cursor position
<Home>	Home key: Moves to the first character of the entry
<End>	End key: Moves to last character of entry
←	Left cursor: Moves the cursor left one character
→	Right cursor: Moves right one character
<Enter>	Enter key: Completes the entry

Actions:

1. Open the workbook **Fox**.

2. Click in cell **B7**. Observe the cell contents in the **Formula Bar**. Click in the **Formula Bar** (the mode indicator on the **Status Bar** now shows **Edit**).

3. Using the features listed above, change **brown** to **red**.

*Note: When editing, the <**Enter**> key must be used to complete the changes.*

4. Move to cell **E7** and change **lazy** to **sleeping**.

5. Move to cell **C10**. Enter a column of four small numbers in **C10**, **C11**, **C12** and **C13**.

6. Enter a formula in **C14** to total the four numbers.

7. Move to cell **C9** and enter another small number. Move back to **C14** and change the formula to include **C9** at the beginning.

8. Close the workbook <u>without</u> saving.

Exercise 27 - In Cell Editing

Guidelines:

As well as editing in the **Formula Bar**, text can be edited directly in a cell: **In Cell Editing**. A cursor is displayed in the cell and the usual movement keys can be used to edit in the cell. The <**Enter**> is still has to be used to end the editing.

Actions:

1.   Start a new workbook and on a blank sheet, type **toda** in cell **A1** and press <**Enter**>.

2.   This is an error which you will now correct. Select cell **A1** and press <**F2**>. A flashing cursor will be displayed in the cell, at the end of the cell contents. Type a letter **y** to complete the spelling of the word and press <**Enter**>.

3.   Select cell **A2** and type **yyesterda**. Complete the cell entry by pressing <**Enter**>.

4.   Double click in cell **A2** to display the flashing cursor. Press <**Home**> to move the cursor to the start of the cell content and then press <**Delete**> to erase the extra letter **y**.

5.   With the cursor still flashing in cell **A2**, press <**End**> to move the cursor to the end of the cell content. Type a letter **y** and press <**Enter**> to make the spelling correct.

6.   Once again, double click to display the cursor in cell **A2**. Click and drag to select **yester** and press <**Delete**>, then <**Enter**>. The word **day** should be left in cell **A2**.

Note: *Any part of a cell's contents can be formatted by clicking and dragging during the edit process. **Formatting** is covered in **Section 6**.*

7.   Close the workbook <u>without</u> saving.

Exercise 28 - Revision

1. Open the workbook **Retail**, which is used to calculate the income and expenditure of a small company.

2. Select cell **A4** and overtype the label **Turnover** with **Income**.

3. Replace the label **Spending** in **A10** with **Expenditure**.

4. Note that the current **Total Net Profit** in cell **N14** is **£77,527**.

5. Replace the value **8.99** in cell **B3** with **9.99** and use the **Fill Handle** to copy the new value into the columns for **February** through to **June**.

6. Delete the contents of cell **B6** and enter a value of **3000** as the cost of **Promotion** for the month of **January**.

7. What is the new value in cell **N14**?

8. Experiment with increasing or reducing any of the values in the Sales, Articles, Stock, Promotion, Advertising, Wages and Overheads rows. See what effect the changes have on the Total Net Profit.

Note: *Always take care not to accidentally overwrite formulas with values.*

9. Close the workbook. Click **No** when prompted to save.

Note: *The answer for this exercise is listed in the **Answer Section** at the end of the guide.*

Section 5

Printing

By the end of this Section you should be able to:

Print Worksheets

Use Print Preview

Change Orientation and Margins

Display and Remove Gridlines

Display and Print Formulas

Display and Print Row and Column Headings

Create and Edit Headers and Footers

Print Part of a Worksheet

Print to Fit a Set Number of Pages

Exercise 29 - Printing

Guidelines:

Printing worksheets produces a hard copy. To print a worksheet, three commands that work together are used:

Print	Controls the print process.
Print Preview	Shows how the worksheet will look when printed page by page. Used prior to printing and after **Page Setup**.
Page Setup	Controls how the worksheet fits the paper by changing the page settings including landscape, portrait, margins, headers and footers, etc. Is used before and after **Print Preview**.

When using **Print Preview** the other commands are available using buttons on the **Ribbon**. The **Print** dialog box also has a **Preview** button.

Actions:

1. Open the workbook **Sick**. This is a list of employees, showing their absences for the year.

Note: Make sure that the appropriate printer is attached to your computer and that it is switched on and is on-line before attempting to print.

2. This is a small worksheet that fits on one piece of paper. Click the **Office Button** and place the cursor over **Print**, 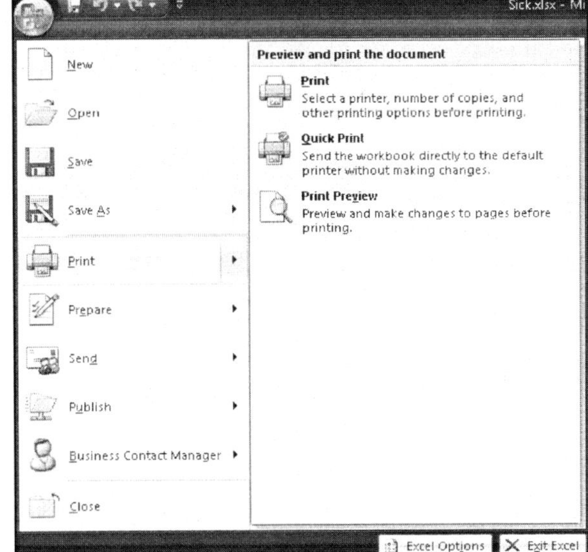.

3. This will display the **Print** options to the right. To automatically start printing with the current settings click the **Quick Print** option to print one copy of the worksheet.

*Note: It is customary to **Print Preview** the worksheet before printing, as it may not fit on the paper and the **Page Layout** tab is used to fit the worksheet to the paper. These topics are covered in the next few exercises.*

4. Close the workbook <u>without</u> saving.

Exercise 30 - Print Preview

Guidelines:

To see how the worksheet will look on paper before printing it, use **Print Preview**. This shows the layout of the worksheet on the paper. All the pages can be viewed. The worksheet can then be printed from within **Print Preview**. Make sure the cell contents - both labels and numbers - are fully displayed before printing.

Actions:

1.   Open the workbook **Hotel**. This is an example of a poorly designed worksheet, made up of several blocks of data.

2.   Click the **Office Button** and point at **Print** (do not click **Print**) and click **Print Preview**.

3.   **Print Preview** is controlled by the command buttons on the **Ribbon**. Scan the pages of **Hotel** by clicking the **Next Page** button.

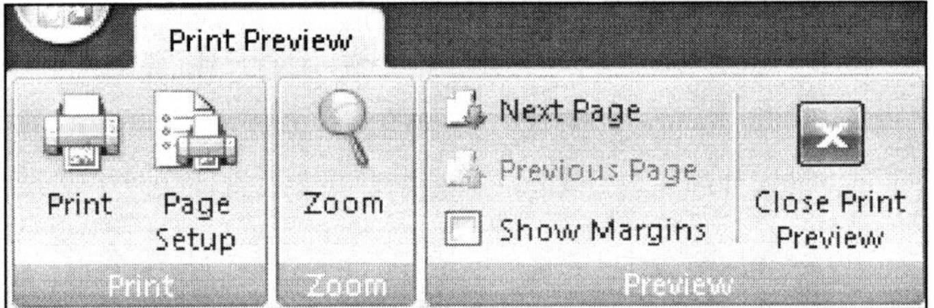

Note: The **Page** and number of pages are displayed on the **Status Bar**.

4.   Move back through the pages by clicking the **Previous Page** button. Display **Page 2**.

5.   The mouse pointer becomes a "magnifying glass" when over the "paper". To zoom in on a particular part of the worksheet, move to the required place and click. Click a second time to zoom out again. Point and click on the **Page number**, bottom centre. Click again to zoom out.

5.   Magnify the title, **Hotel.xlsx**, top centre and zoom out again. Experiment with zooming in and out.

6.   Click the **Close Print Preview** button to close **Print Preview** and return to the worksheet.

7.   Close the workbook <u>without</u> saving.

Exercise 31 - Page Setup

Guidelines:

Page Setup allows the appearance of the printed worksheet to be modified.

Actions:

1.   Open the workbook **Company**.

2.   To preview the workbook, select the **Office Button** display the **Print** options and click **Print Preview**. The worksheet stretches over two portrait pages.

3.   Click the **Page Setup** button from within **Print Preview**.

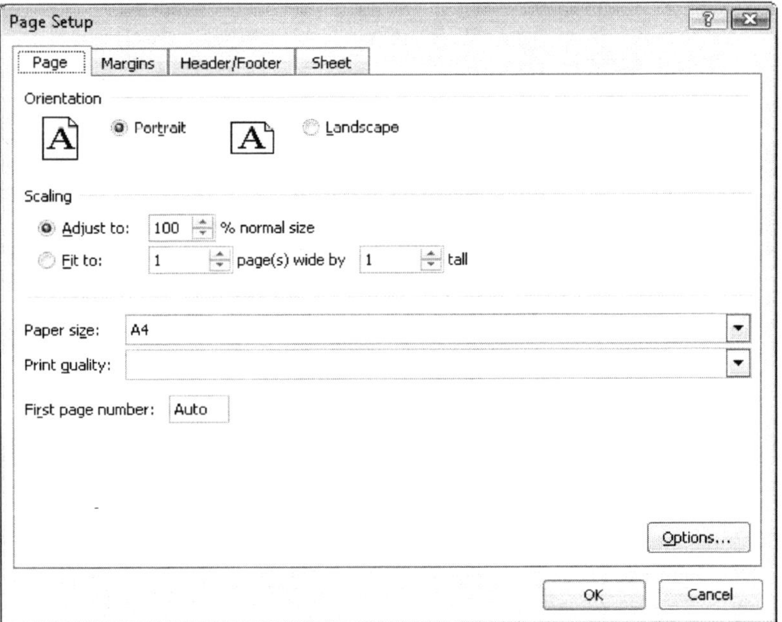

Page Setup with *Page* tab displayed.

4.   The **Page Setup** dialog box has four option tabs, for changing the **Page**, **Margins**, **Header/Footer** and **Sheet** options.

5.   Click the **Page** tab, if it is not selected and view the options.

6.   Click on the other tabs to view their options then click the **Cancel** button, and click **Close Print Preview** to return to the worksheet.

7.   Leave the workbook open for the next exercise.

Exercise 32 - Portrait and Landscape

Guidelines:

The orientation of pages can be changed using the **Orientation** button in the **Page Setup** group on the **Page Layout** tab. The orientation can be **Portrait,**

, or **Landscape,** .

Actions:

1. The workbook **Company** should still be open from the previous exercise, if not open it.

2. Display the **Page Layout** tab.

3. In the **Page Setup** group, click **Orientation** and select **Landscape**. This turns the paper through ninety degrees (short and wide).

4. To check how the worksheet will print now, click the **Office Button** and from the **Print** option, select

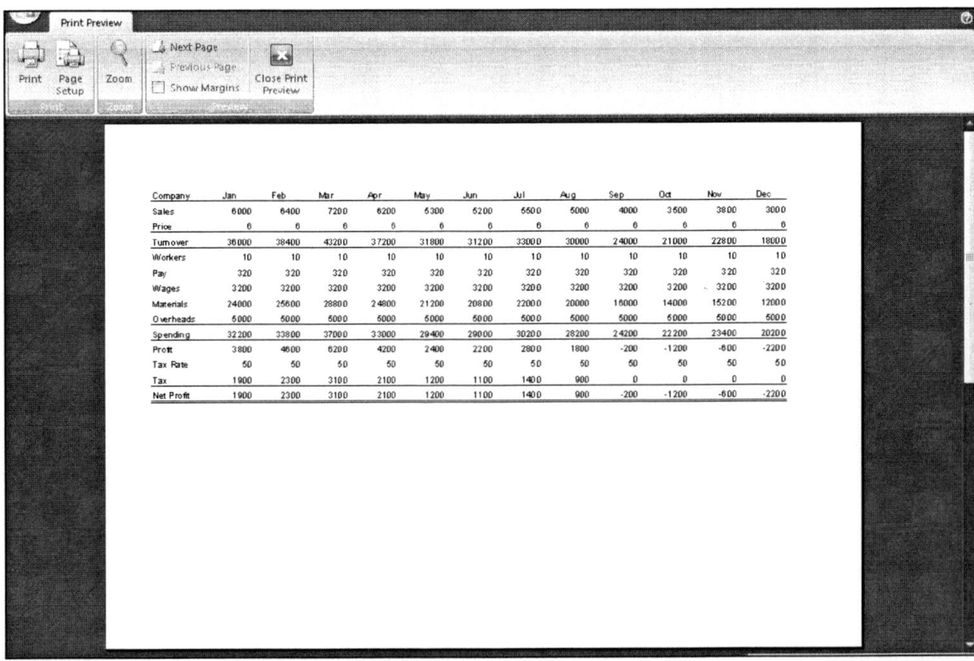

Company	Jan	Feb	Mar	Apr	May	Jun	Jul	Aug	Sep	Oct	Nov	Dec
Sales	6000	6400	7200	6200	5300	5200	5500	5000	4000	3500	3800	3000
Price	6	6	6	6	6	6	6	6	6	6	6	6
Turnover	36000	38400	43200	37200	31800	31200	33000	30000	24000	21000	22800	18000
Workers	10	10	10	10	10	10	10	10	10	10	10	10
Pay	320	320	320	320	320	320	320	320	320	320	320	320
Wages	3200	3200	3200	3200	3200	3200	3200	3200	3200	3200	3200	3200
Materials	24000	25600	28800	24800	21200	20800	22000	20000	16000	14000	15200	12000
Overheads	5000	5000	5000	5000	5000	5000	5000	5000	5000	5000	5000	5000
Spending	32200	33800	37000	33000	29400	29000	30200	28200	24200	22200	23400	20200
Profit	3800	4600	6200	4200	2400	2200	2800	1800	-200	-1200	-600	-2200
Tax Rate	50	50	50	50	50	50	50	50	50	50	50	50
Tax	1900	2300	3100	2100	1200	1100	1400	900	0	0	0	0
Net Profit	1900	2300	3100	2100	1200	1100	1400	900	-200	-1200	-600	-2200

*Note: The spreadsheet now fits on to a single page except for the **Total** column.*

5. Worksheets can be printed from within **Print Preview** by clicking the **Print** button. Click the **Print** button but because the worksheet covers 2 pages, click **Cancel** to close the dialog box without printing.

6. Leave the workbook open for the next exercise.

Exercise 33 - Margins

Guidelines:

Page Margins can be changed using the **Margins** button in the **Page Setup** group of the **Page Layout** tab. A menu shows four standard settings and a **Custom Margins** option. The spreadsheet can be centred horizontally and/or vertically on the page.

Actions:

1. The workbook **Company** should still be open from the previous exercise, if not open it.

2. Display the **Page Layout** tab and click the **Margins** button.

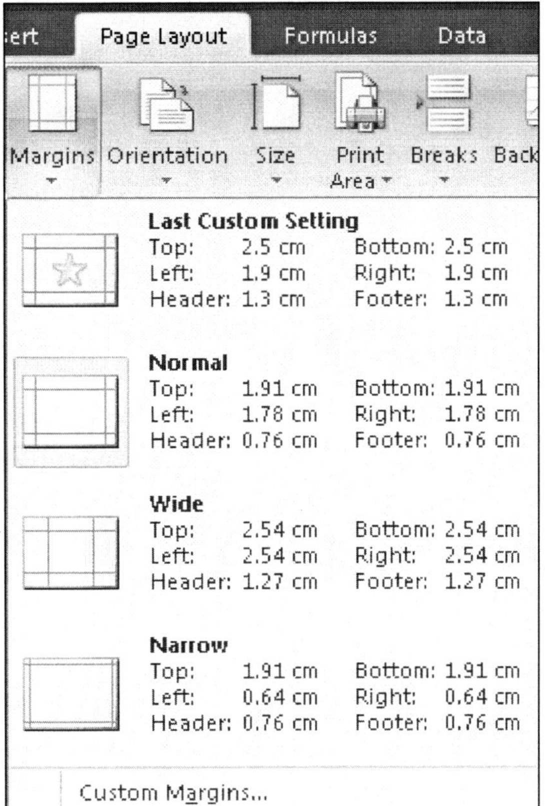

3. At the bottom of the menu, click **Custom Margins**.

4. This opens the **Page Setup** dialog box with the **Margins** tab displayed.

continued over

Exercise 33 - Continued

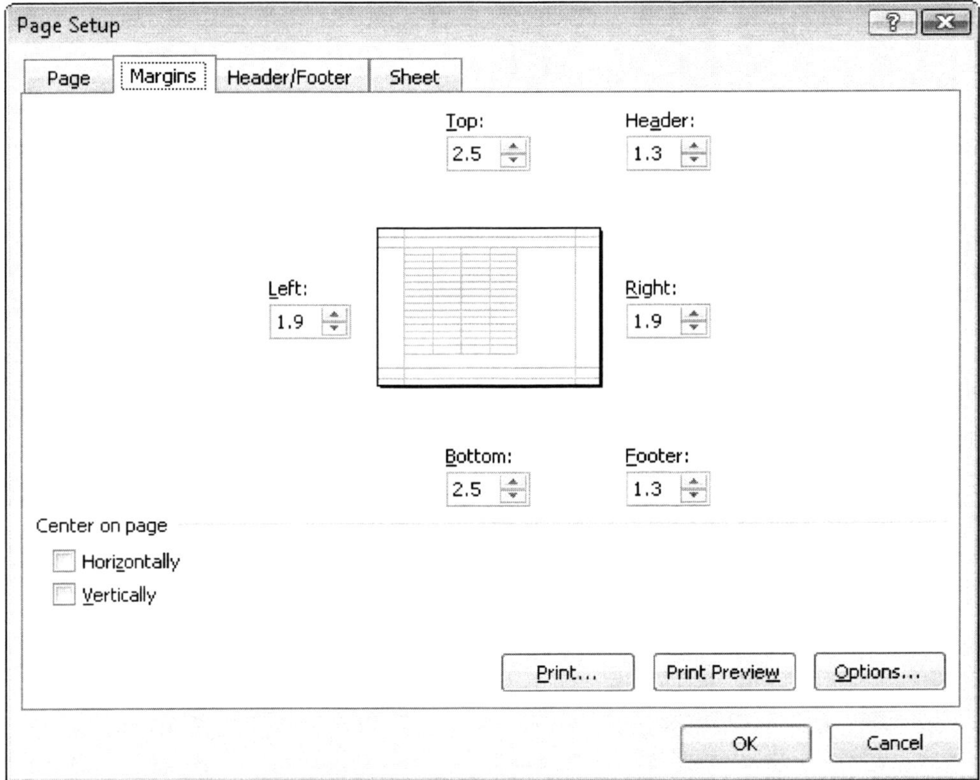

5.   Reduce the **Left** and **Right** margins to **1.4** by clicking once on the down arrow, ⬍, next to the current size.

*Note: Reducing **Margins** increases the area on which to print.*

6.   Click **Print Preview** to see the worksheet with the new settings.

7.   It still does not fit on to one page. Click the **Page Setup** button and click on the **Page** tab.

8.   A worksheet can be scaled to fit to any number of pages. Select the **Fit to** option, under **Scaling**, which will be **1 page wide by 1 tall** automatically.

*Note: The spreadsheet can also be scaled to a certain percentage of the original using this feature. When using **Fit to**, remember that it will fit to the number of pages specified and may be so small that the worksheet cannot be read. Always use **Print Preview**, therefore, before printing.*

9.   Click OK to return to **Print Preview**. Check the **Status Bar** for the number of Pages, it should be **Page 1 of 1**.

10.   Print a copy of the spreadsheet, then save the workbook as **Company2**.

11.   Close the workbook.

Exercise 34 - Display and Print Formulas

Guidelines:

When a cell contains a formula, the result of the formula rather than the formula itself is displayed in the cell. This is because normally the value is the required result in a worksheet. However, it is possible to display formulas on a worksheet rather than the results of the formulas. This is very useful when checking for errors on a worksheet.

To print formulas it is only necessary to display them and then print as normal, but usually it is especially important to check formulas are displayed in full before attempting to print. Usually when formulas are printed, the row and column headings are printed as well. To make the checking easier, the gridlines can also be printed.

Actions:

1.   Open the workbook **House**.

2.   To display all the formulas on the screen, click **Show Formulas** 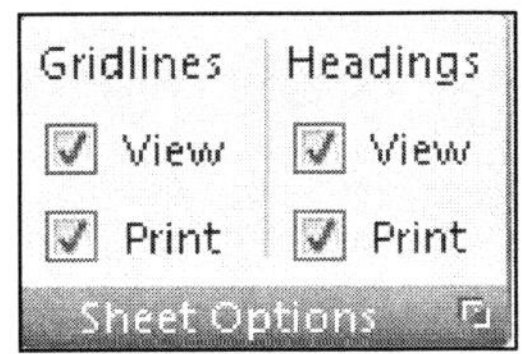 from the **Formulas** tab. The formulas are now shown.

Note: _Alternatively, and much more quickly, it is possible to switch between formulas and their results by pressing **<Ctrl `>**, i.e. **Ctrl** and the key to the left of 1._

3.   Switch to the results and then switch back to the formulas using the quick key press method.

4.   If the formulas are to be printed, it is normal to display the row and column headings and the gridlines with the formulas so they can be checked. Display the **Page Layout** tab and then check **Print** under **Gridlines** and **Print** under **Headings**, in the **Sheet Options** group.

5.   Use **Print Preview** to see the results.

6.   View the pages and then close **Print Preview**.

7.   On the **Page Layout** tab uncheck **Print** under **Gridlines** and **Print** under **Headings** to stop the **Headings** and **Gridlines** from being printed.

8.   Click the **Show Formulas** button on the **Formulas** tab to remove the displayed formulas.

9.   Save the workbook as **House2** and leave the workbook open.

Exercise 35 - Gridlines

Guidelines:

As well as adding and removing **Gridlines** from a printed spreadsheet, they can also be removed from the screen using the **Gridlines** options in the **Sheet Options** group on the **Page Layout** tab.

Actions:

1. The workbook **House2** should still be open from the previous exercise, if not open it.

2. To remove the gridlines from the spreadsheet, on screen, select the **Page Layout** tab.

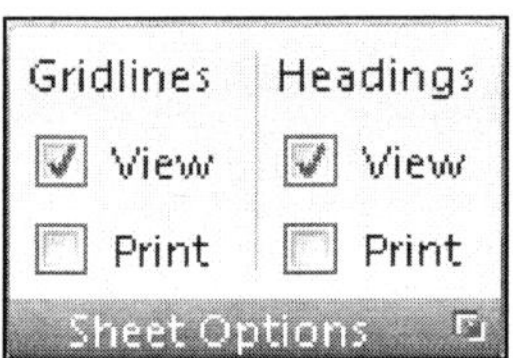

3. Look at the **Sheet Options** group. **Gridlines** has **View** checked and **Print** not. This means that the **Gridlines** are displayed on screen but not printed. Uncheck **View** under **Gridlines** to remove them from the screen.

Note: *Lines which have been added manually will still appear on the screen. **Gridlines** can still be printed if they do not appear on the screen, by checking **Print** under **Gridlines**.*

	A	B	C	D	E
1	House Finance	Jan	Feb	Mar	Apr
2	Pay	1185	1185	1185	1250
3	Other Income	0	0	0	0
4	Total Income	1185	1185	1185	1250
5	Rent	200	200	200	200
6	Holidays	0	0	0	500
7	Leisure	125	200	175	100
8	Electricity	89	0	0	140
9	Gas	150	0	0	200
10	Telephone	0	76	0	0
11	Car	0	56	291	0
12	Petrol	60	75	60	75
13	Food	240	260	200	240
14	Others	55	45	100	65
15	Total Expenses	919	912	1026	1520
16	Savings	266	539	698	428
17					

*Part of the worksheet without **Gridlines** displayed on screen*

4. Display the gridlines again.

5. Save the workbook using the same filename and close it.

Exercise 36 - Headers and Footers

Guidelines:

Headers and **Footers** are lines of text at the top/bottom of every printed page. **Automatic Fields** are codes which insert page numbers, date, time, etc. into headers and footers easily.

Note: *Be careful when using **Headers** and **Footers** as the worksheet can occupy the same space if the **Top** and **Bottom** margins have been reduced.*

Actions:

1. Open the workbook **Survey**. Preview the workbook. It has a title on page one but the other 4 pages just contain data. Close the preview.

2. Display the **Insert** tab and click the **Header & Footer** button. This displays the **Header** on the worksheet and the **Design** tab within **Header & Footer Tools**. The view is **Page Layout**.

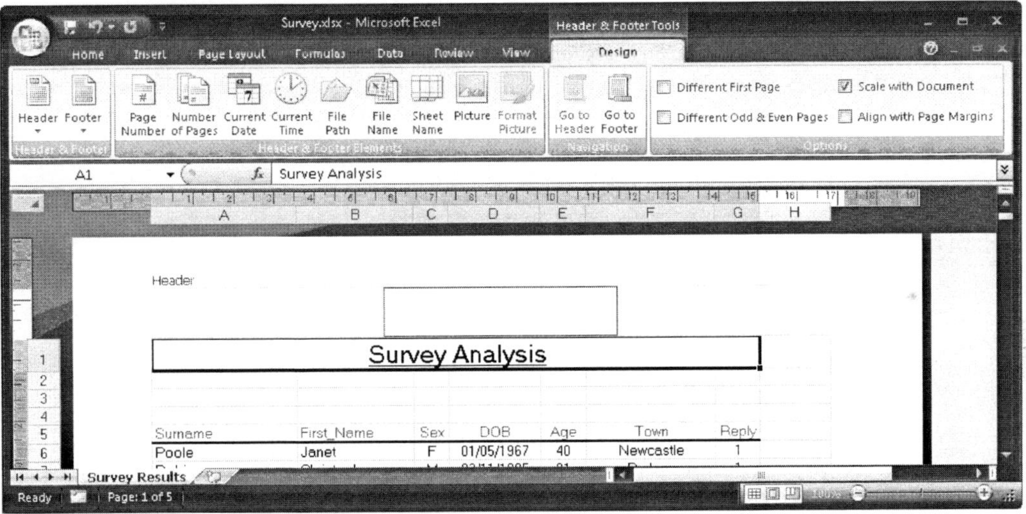

3. Examine the **Design** tab to see the available tools when dealing with **Headers and Footers**.

4. The cursor is placed in the central section. Type the title **Survey Analysis**. Any text can be entered by typing in any of the sections; left, centre or right.

5. There are various buttons on the **Design** tab that place field codes into **Headers and Footers** and these are covered when adding a **Footer**.

6. Scroll down the worksheet to see the header on the other pages. The title on row 1 of the worksheet is now duplicated by the **Header**. On page two only the header is displayed.

Note: *When adding a title choose between using a cell on the worksheet or a Header.*

continued over

                                    © CiA Training Ltd 2007

Exercise 36 - Continued

7.   Click on the **Header** and format it to be **18pt** and **underline**, using the **Home** tab. The two titles match.

8.   The tile on row 1 is now surplus. Click on cell **A1** and remove the cell's contents.

9.   Click in the header. Click the **Go to Footer** button, on the **Design** tab to display the blank footer.

10.   Click in the **Left section** and then click the **Current Date** button, this places the field code **&[Date]** in the box. This code displays the current date.

11.   Click in the **Center section**. The left section now displays the codes as text.

12.   Type **Page** (followed by a space) and click the **Page Number** button, . *Excel* places the field code **&[Page]** in the box.

13.   Click in the **Right section** and click the **File Name** button, . The field code is **&[File]**. This identifies the printout, it displays the workbook name.

14.   Scroll the worksheet to check each part of the **Footer**. Check the pages.

| Morgan | Deidre | F | 05/08/1968 | 38 | Sunderland |
| Thompson | Trevor | M | 17/08/1970 | 36 | Washington |

| 04/05/2007 | Page 2 | Survey.xlsx |

*A sample **Footer** showing **Page 2***

15.   To change the view back to normal display the **View** tab and click the **Normal** button.

Note: *Click the **Page Layout** button on the **View** tab to show the headers and footers on the worksheet.*

16.   Preview the worksheet to see the effects of the headers and footers. View all 5 pages. Close the preview.

17.   Save the workbook as **HeaderFooter** and close it.

Note: *Headers and footers can also be created using **Header/Footer** tab within the **Page Setup** dialog box.*

Exercise 37 - Printing a Selection

Guidelines:

Part of a worksheet, a **Selection**, can be printed, instead of the whole sheet.

Actions:

1. Open workbook **House**.

2. Display all of the formulas on the spreadsheet by clicking the **Show Formulas** button on the **Formulas** tab.

3. Change the orientation of the page to **Landscape**.

4. To print part of a worksheet (a **selection**) highlight the range **A1:E16**.

5. To select the **Total** column as part of the range, scroll across to column **N** and while holding the <Ctrl> key, highlight the range **N1:N16**.

6. Click the **Office Button** and click **Print** and under **Print what** choose the **Selection** option.

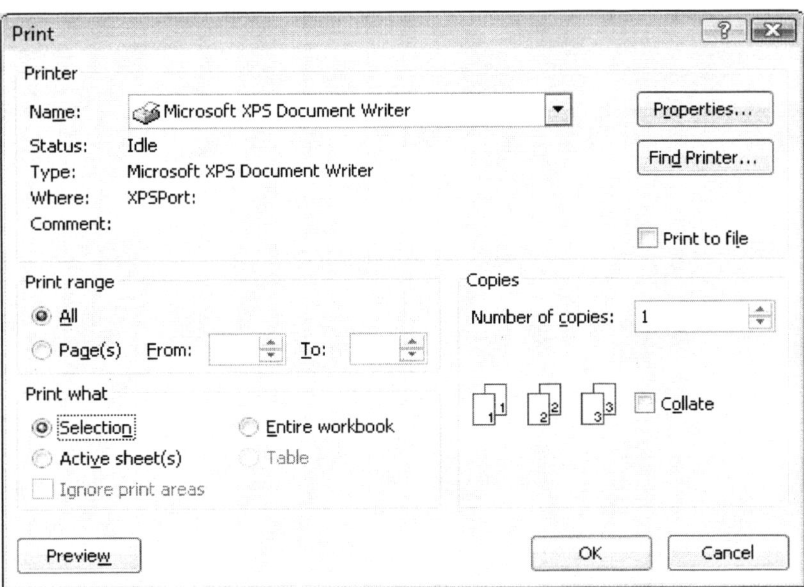

Note: *The selection can be previewed using the* **Preview** *button in the* **Print** *dialog box, but only after the* **Selection** *option has been chosen.*

7. Click ⟨ OK ⟩ to print.

Note: *When <Ctrl> is used to select multiple ranges, the different ranges are always printed out on separate pages. Alternatively, the different ranges can simply be printed one after the other, eliminating the need to use <Ctrl>.*

8. Close the workbook <u>without</u> saving.

Exercise 38 - Revision

1.   Open the workbook **Retail**.

2.   Obtain a printed copy of the first six months.

3.   Alter the **Page Setup** for printing to the following:

- Use landscape orientation.

- Margins   top   2 cm

             bottom   2 cm

             left   2 cm

             right   2 cm

- Insert your name into the header.

- For the footer add an automatic date field, page number and filename.

4.   Print a copy of the whole worksheet.

5.   Close the workbook **Retail** <u>without</u> saving.

6.   Open the workbook **Hotel98**.

7.   Delete the contents of cell **C1**.

8.   Print a copy of the worksheet.

9.   Fit the worksheet to print on one landscape page.

10.   Print another copy of the worksheet.

11.   Close the workbook <u>without</u> saving.

Section 6

Formatting Cells

By the end of this Section you should be able to:

Format Numbers

Enter and Format Dates and Times

Use Alignment

Add Borders

Use Wrap Text

Merge Cells

Rotate Text

Exercise 39 - General Formatting

Guidelines:

Cells can be **Formatted** in a number of ways. Formatting cells in a worksheet improves its appearance and makes it easier to read and use. Text and cells in a spreadsheet can be emphasised in *Excel* using **Bold**, **Italic** and **Underline**, as well as changing the **Font**, **Font Size** and **Font Colour**.

House Style refers to the guidelines specified for the production of a document. These include paper size and orientation, margins, headers and footers, text styles (font and size) and instructions on the positioning and formatting of objects.

Actions:

1.   On a blank worksheet, enter your name in cell **H2** and press **<Enter>**.

2.   To make the text **Bold**, with cell **H2** as the active cell, click the **Bold** button, **B** on the **Home** tab. When a feature is in operation, note that the button has an orange background.

3.   Click the **Italic** button, *I*, and then the **Underline** button, **U**, to italicise and underline the already bold text. Click away from the cell to see the results more clearly.

Note: A range of cells can be formatted at the same time by highlighting the whole range first.

4.   Make the cell **H2** active again.

5.   To change the font, click the drop down list in the **Font** box, in the **Font** group on the **Home** tab, Calibri.

6.   There are over 200 fonts to choose from, scroll down list and view the interactive change to the cell. Select **Algerian** font from the list (or any other if this is not available).

7.   The font size can be changed easily by clicking on the drop down **Font Size** box, 11. Scroll down the list to see the change, then select **14**.

Note: The row height changes automatically when the size is increased, if the row height has not been changed manually.

8.   Another useful feature to make text stand out in spreadsheets is font colour. With **H2** still active, click on the **Font Color** drop down button, **A**. Choose any colour from the palette to see the colour of the font change in the cell.

9.   Close the workbook <u>without</u> saving.

Exercise 40 - Format Cells

Guidelines:

Formatting can change the look of text, text alignment, text colour, number formats, font style, font size, border lines and cell colour.

Formatting can be added to a worksheet by either clicking buttons on the **Ribbon** or by using key presses.

Actions:

1. Start a new workbook. The **Ribbon** displays the **Home** tab by default.

2. The groups on the **Home** tab, show the various different formatting options. Check each one in turn with reference to the list below:

- The **Clipboard** group allows you to move/copy/paste items in different cells and the **Office Clipboard Task Pane** can be displayed from here.

- The **Font** group, controls how the contents look.

- The **Alignment** group, controls how the contents are positioned in the cells.

- The **Number** group allows formatting of numbers, dates, times and percentages, etc.

- The **Styles** group, controls the lines around the cells, the background cell colour and cell shading. This group also allows you to add conditional formatting.

- The **Cells** tab, controls inserting/deleting of cells and changes the row height or column width, organises sheets and also protects and hides cells.

- The **Editing** tab, controls the editing features as well as **Sort & Filter** and **Find & Replace**.

3. Close the workbook <u>without</u> saving.

Exercise 41 - Format Number

Guidelines:

Numbers can be formatted to be displayed in a variety of ways, such as currency, percentages, etc.

The number formats are as follows:

Type	Description
General	No specific number format
Number	Plain number formats
Currency	Pound signs and decimal places
Accounting	Specialised accounting formats
Short Date	Displays the short date
Long Date	Displays the long date
Time	Displays the time
Percentage	Multiplied by 100 (followed by %)
Fraction	Decimals expressed as fractions
Scientific	Exponent / Mantissa format
More Number Formats	Opens the **Format Cells** dialogue box with more options.

There are also five number formatting buttons in the **Number** group.

Accounting Number Format,

Percentage Style,

Comma Style,

Increase Decimal

Decrease Decimal

Actions:

1.   Open the workbook **Cars**.

2.   Select the range **F2:F11**.

continued over

Exercise 41 - Continued

3. Click the dialog box launcher in the **Number** group on the **Home** tab. The **Number** tab in the **Format Cells** dialog box is displayed by default.

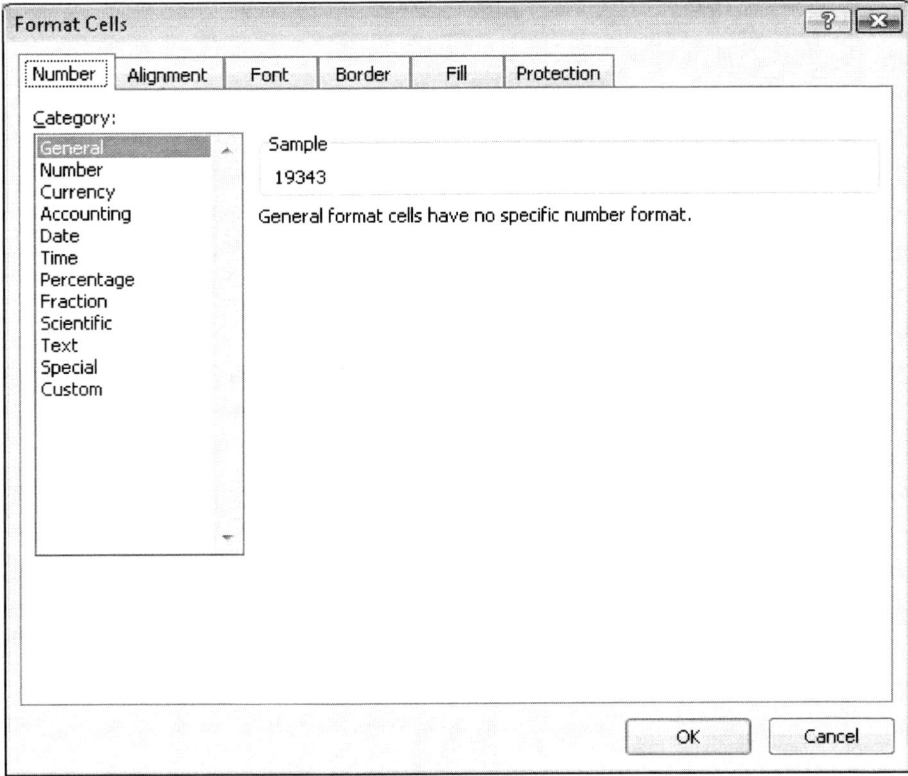

4. Click on each of the different categories to see the types of number formatting available, then select the **Number** category.

5. Click to place a tick in the **Use 1000 Separator (,)** check box and ensure that **2** is displayed in the **Decimal places** setting. Click **OK** and observe the changes in appearance that the formatting has made.

6. Identify the **Increase Decimal**, and **Decrease Decimal**, buttons in the **Number** group. With the same range of cells still selected, click the **Decrease Decimal** button, twice. The values for **Mileage** should now be displayed with a comma separating the thousands, and with no decimal places.

Note: *After applying number formats, cells may display ########. This means that the number is too big to be displayed in the cell, although the cell content remains correct. This can be corrected by widening the column, this is covered in the next Section.*

7. Close the workbook <u>without</u> saving.

Exercise 42 - Date and Time

Guidelines:

Date and **Time** are stored as numbers. The **Date** is a number representing the number of days since 1 January 1900 (years between 00 and 29 entered with two numbers are treated as being after 2000 e.g. 18 is 2018). The **Time** is a decimal, as part of a day.

Both the **Date** and **Time** can be displayed in various formats including numbers and text.

Actions:

1.   Start a new workbook.

2.   In cell **B2** enter your date of birth (in the form of 31/12/06). Press **<Enter>**. The date is displayed in the default date format, dd/mm/yyyy.

3.   Click back in cell **B2**. The cells may now be shown as **Date** 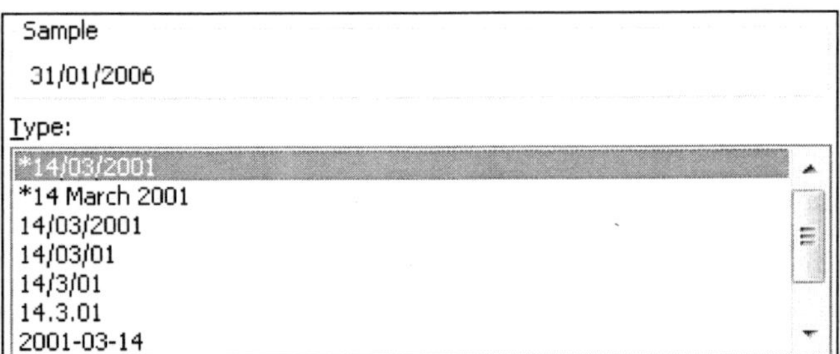 in the **Number Format** box in the **Number** group.

4.   Click the **Number** group dialog box launcher to display the **Format Cells** dialog box. **Date** is selected in the **Category** section. Select each format from within **Type**. A preview is available in the **Sample** box within the dialog box.

```
Sample
  31/01/2006

Type:
*14/03/2001
*14 March 2001
14/03/2001
14/03/01
14/3/01
14.3.01
2001-03-14
```

5.   Select any of the **14 March 2001** formats and click **OK**.

6.   Click in cell **B4** and enter today's date by pressing **<Ctrl ;>**. This is the quick key press to enter the current date. Press **<Enter>** to complete the entry.

7.   With cell **B4** active, repeat Step **4** and then select a different format.

8.   Click in cell **B6** and enter the current time by pressing **<Ctrl Shift ;>**. Press **<Enter>**. Click back in cell **B6**.

9.   To change the format of the time, display the **Format Number** dialog box and from the **Date** category, select a suitable time format. Click **OK**.

10. Close the workbook <u>without</u> saving.

Exercise 43 - Alignment

Guidelines:

Aligning means changing the position of cell contents within the cell relative to its edges. Contents can be aligned horizontally or vertically and the orientation (rotation of text) can also be changed.

Actions:

1. Open the workbook **Sandwiches2** (saved in **Exercise 18**).

2. Select the range **B3:E3** and click the **Center** button, 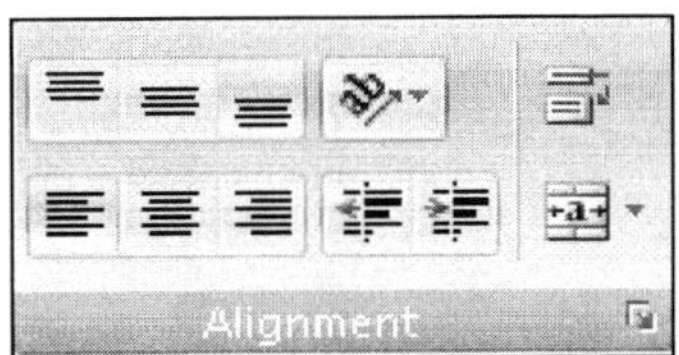, from the **Alignment** group on the **Home** tab to centre the labels in the centre of the cells, horizontally.

3. Save the changes and close the workbook.

4. Open the workbook **Climate** and select the range of cells **B4:K4**.

*The **Alignment** group on the **Home** tab*

5. Settings for the **Vertical** alignment are shown on the top row of this group. The **Horizontal** alignment is shown on the second row. Select **Center** from each.

6. The values in the range are now centred vertically and horizontally within the cells. Click anywhere away from the selected range to see the effect more clearly.

7. Save the workbook as **Climate2** and close it.

Exercise 44 - Wrap Text

Guidelines:

Wrap Text is used to fit data into cells without widening the columns. The row height is increased automatically, if not manually set previously.

Actions:

1. Open the workbook **Fruit Sales**.

2. With the active cell as the title in **A1**, click the **Wrap Text** button, from the **Alignment** group on the **Home** tab.

3. The text now fits in column **A**, but has taken two lines. The row height is adjusted automatically.

Note: If the row height had been set manually, then as with adding a larger font, the row height would have to be adjusted manually (described in the next section).

4. **Print Preview** the worksheet.

5. Close **Print Preview**.

6. Save the workbook as **Fruit Sales2**.

7. Leave the workbook open for the next exercise.

Exercise 45 - Merge Cells

Guidelines:

Merge cells is used to combine two or more cells into one. It is very useful when creating, for example, an invoice or placing a title across several columns.

Actions:

1. The workbook **Fruit Sales2** should be open from the previous exercise, if not open it.

2. Unwrap the text of the title by clicking the **Wrap Text** button and change the font size to **20**.

3. Highlight the range **A1:E1** and click the **Merge and Center** button, 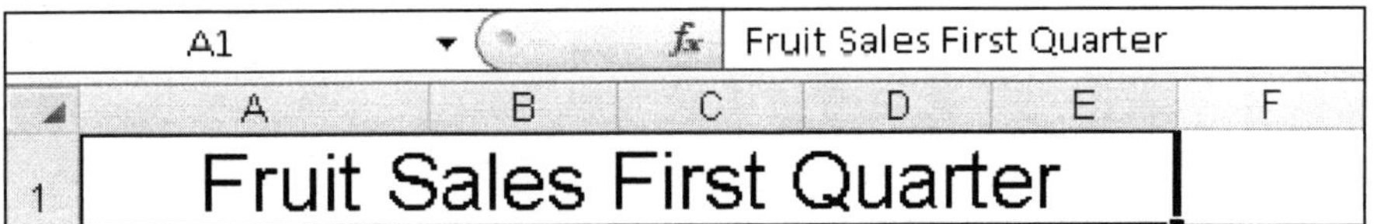, from the **Alignment** group to merge the cells **A1** to **E1**.

4. The cells are **Merged** to make one cell, **A1**.

5. To remove the merging, click the **Merge & Center** button, again.

6. Make **Sheet2** active. This blank sheet is to be used for experimenting with **Merge cells**.

7. Cells can also be merged vertically. Select the range **B2:B6** and click the **Merge and Center** button.

Note: *Even though the merging is vertical, the centring is still horizontal. If this alignment is not required, then use the alignment buttons to change it.*

8. Enter **Fred** in cell **B2**. Merge the range **D2:F2** and enter **Fred** in **D2**.

9. Cells can be merged horizontally and vertically. Highlight the range **D4:F6** and click the **Merge and Centre** button. Enter **Fred** in cell **D4**.

10. Click on cell **D4** and click **Middle Align** to add centre vertical alignment to place **Fred** in the centre of the merged range **D4:F6**.

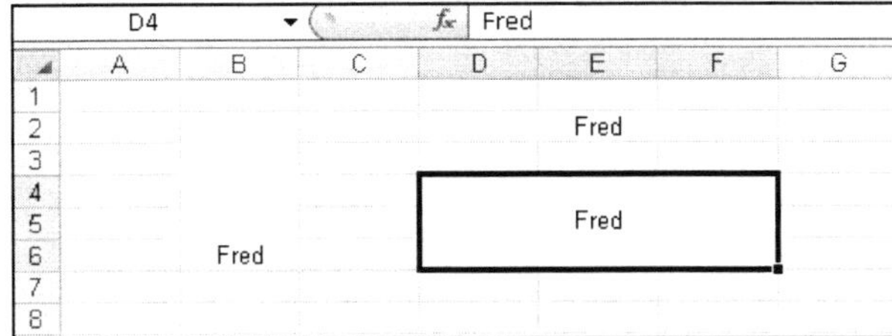

11. Click on cell **D2** and remove the cell merging.

12. Save the workbook and leave it open for the next exercise.

Exercise 46 - Text Orientation

Guidelines:

Cell contents can be displayed vertically or at any angle in the cell. This is called **Orientation**.

Actions:

1. The workbook **Fruit Sales2** should be open from the previous exercise, if not open it.

2. On **Sheet2**, click on cell **D4** and click the **Orientation** button in the **Alignment** group. The menu controls the angle at which the cell contents are displayed.

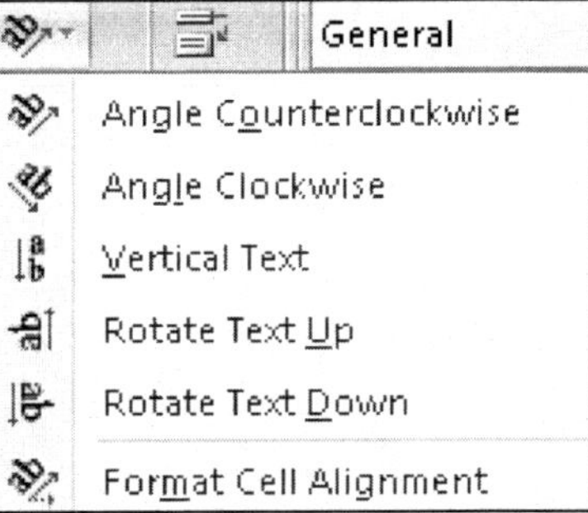

3. To rotate the contents, select **Format Cell Alignment** and either type a number of degrees in the **Degrees** box, use the **Degrees** spinner, drag the line round in the picture or click on the markers around the semicircle. Change the angle of the text to **30** degrees, using any method.

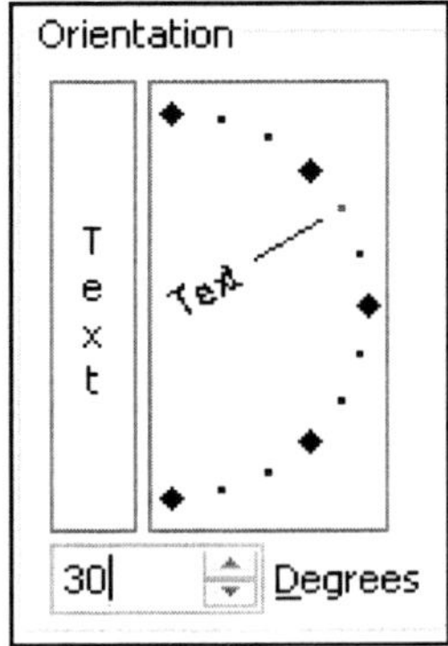

4. Click ⌊ OK ⌋.

5. Click on cell **B2** and change the contents so that they read vertically down, letter by letter.

6. Print a copy of the worksheet, centred horizontally.

7. Save the workbook using the same file name and leave it open for the next exercise.

Exercise 47 - Borders

Guidelines:

Borders are lines, thicker than gridlines, around the edges of the cells. Options are available on the style of line used, including thin, thick, dotted lines, etc. The lines may be put around the outside or inside of the range, or on any edge. The colour of the lines can also be changed.

Actions:

1. The workbook **Fruit Sales2** should still be open from the previous exercise. If not, open it.

2. On **Sheet1** select the range **A3:E11**. Click the **Borders** button drop down in the **Font** group as shown below.

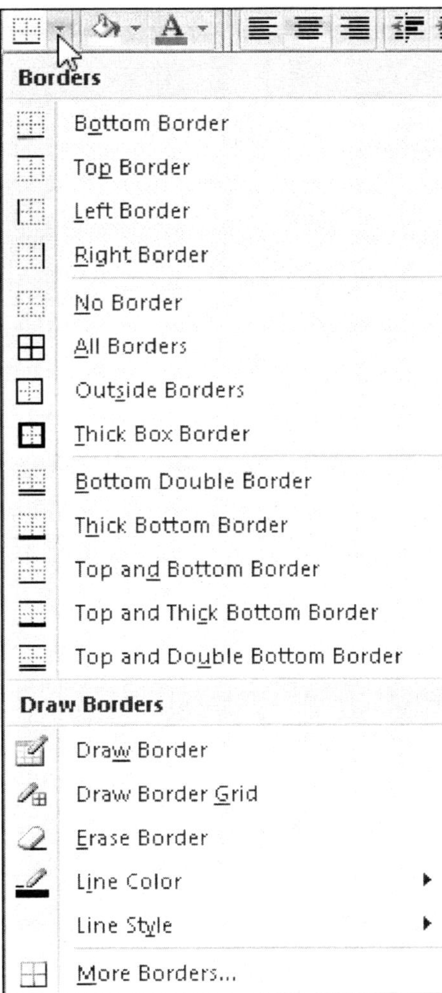

3. Select **All Borders** to add lines to the whole range. Click away to view the results.

Note: Clicking on the button itself applies the last border chosen to the current cells.

continued over

Exercise 47 - Continued

4.   Click **Undo** to remove the lines.

5.   Highlight the range **A3:E11** again, if not already highlighted. Click the **Border** button drop down and click **More Borders** to display the **Border** tab in the **Format Cells** dialog box.

6.   Under **Style**, select one of the **dotted** lines, in **Color** choose **Red**, finally select **Outline** under the **Presets**.

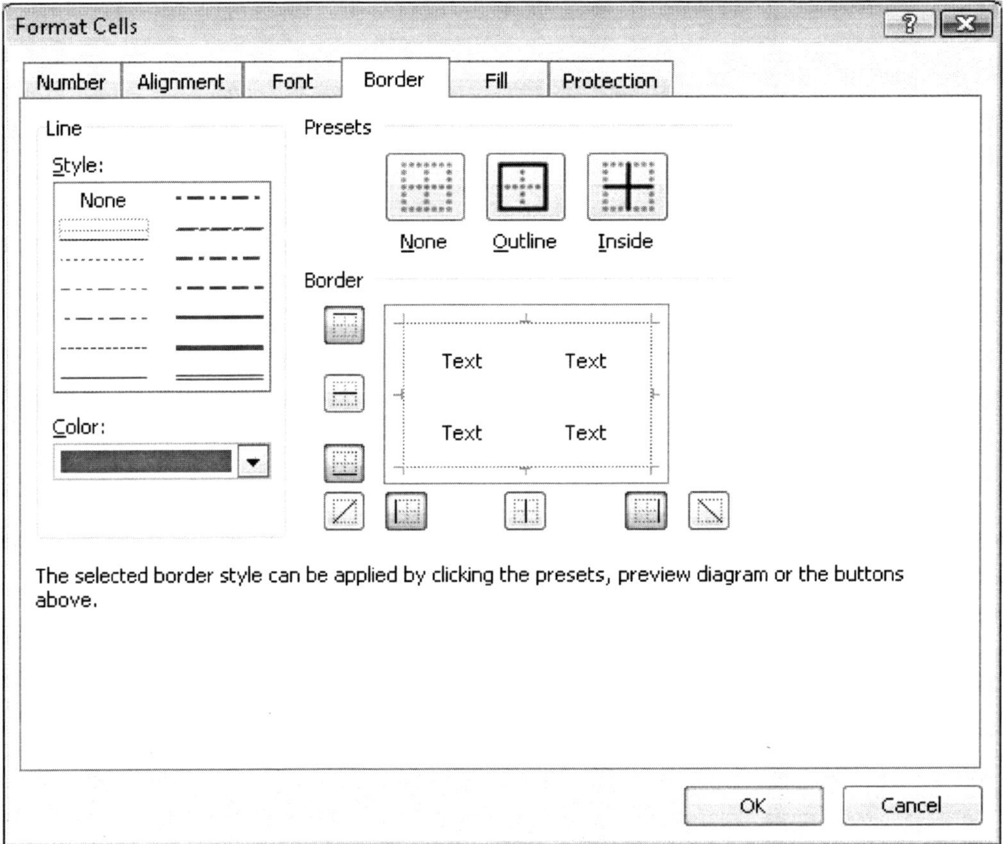

Note: **Presets** *are always selected after the* **Line Style** *and* **Color** *selections.*

7.   To apply the formats, click on **OK**. Click away to view the effect.

8.   Practise adding borders to ranges of cells, using the **Border** buttons and by clicking on the **Preview** diagram, in the **Format Cells** dialog box.

9.   Save the workbook and close it.

Exercise 48 - Revision

1. Open the workbook **Interest Rates**.

2. In cell **B15**, enter the current time, using a key press.

3. In cell **A15**, type **Start**.

4. The amounts are right aligned, select the range **A4:A11** and centre the range.

5. Select the range **B3:E3** and format this range as **Percentages** using the **%** button.

6. Select the range **B4:E11** and format as **Currency** with **2** decimal places, with **£** signs added.

7. Change the font of the title in **A1** to **Impact** and change the size to **18**.

8. Add a thick **Blue** outline to the range **A3:E11**.

9. Add **Bold** to the range **A3:E3** and a thin **Blue** line to the bottom of this range.

10. Change the text colour of the range **A3:A11** to **Red**.

11. In cell **A16** type **Finish**.

12. In cell **A17** type **Elapsed time** and in cell **B17** enter the formula to subtract the two times **=B16-B15**. This results in **######**.

13. In cell **B16**, enter the current time with a key press. The formula now displays the time taken to complete this exercise.

14. Obtain a horizontally centred printed copy of the worksheet display on one page only.

15. Save the worksheet as **Interest Rates2** and close it.

Section 7

Formatting Worksheets

By the end of this Section you should be able to:

Change Column Widths

Hide and Display Rows and Columns

Exercise 49 - Changing Column Widths

Guidelines:

Column widths are changed to accommodate the contents of the cells within the columns. A column width is measured using the average number of digits in the standard font, the default is **8.43** and the number of pixels **64**.

Actions:

1. Open the workbook **Formatting Section**, created earlier. As column **C** contains no data, the titles in column **B** are displayed in full.

2. In cell **C3** enter the heading **Page No**.

3. In column **C**, enter the page numbers as below:

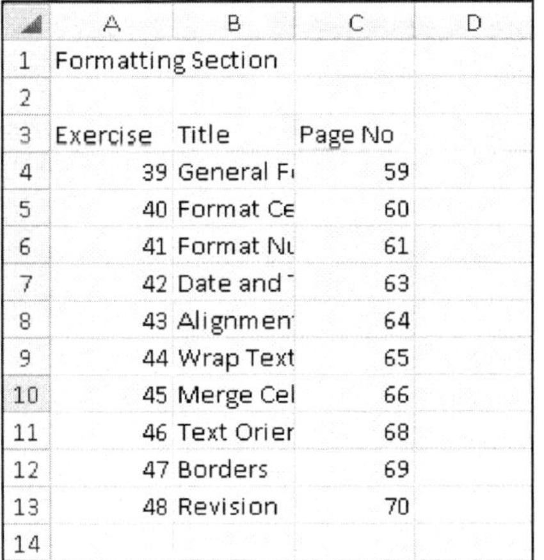

	A	B	C	D
1	Formatting Section			
2				
3	Exercise	Title	Page No	
4	39	General Fi	59	
5	40	Format Ce	60	
6	41	Format Nu	61	
7	42	Date and '	63	
8	43	Alignmen'	64	
9	44	Wrap Text	65	
10	45	Merge Cel	66	
11	46	Text Orier	68	
12	47	Borders	69	
13	48	Revision	70	
14				

4. Adding the page numbers has truncated most of the titles in column **B**. Move the pointer to the border between column **B** and column **C** in the column **Title Bar**. The pointer should change shape to a double arrow, ✛, the **Adjust Cursor**.

B	✛	C

5. Click the mouse button and, with the button still pressed, drag the column border to the right. Drag the column width to **18.00** or **131** pixels. Release the mouse button.

6. An alternative way to change a column width is to use the menus. Click on any cell in column **C**. Click **Format** from the **Cells** group on the **Home** tab, select **Column Width**. Enter a column width of **3**, then click [OK].

7. Move the mouse pointer to the border between column **C** and column **D** in the column headings. Double click the mouse. The width of column **C** is automatically adjusted to the widest entry in the column. This is the easiest way of changing the widths of individual columns.

8. Save the workbook as **Formatting Section2** and close it.

Exercise 50 - Hiding Rows and Columns

Guidelines:

Rows and/or **Columns** of sensitive data can be hidden. For example, in a spreadsheet used for accounts you may want to hide a column containing salary details. Any calculations contained on the sheet are unaffected by hiding.

Actions:

1. Open the workbook **Payroll**.

2. Click on K in the column headings to highlight column **K**, which is a **Spare** column for any new staff. Click the **Format** button in **Cells** group, select **Hide & Unhide** and select **Hide Columns**. Column **K** has now been hidden.

	A	J	L	M	N
1	*Payroll*	Harris	Nichols	Chapman	Total
2	Hourly Rate	£2.00	£1.50	£1.50	£43.25
3	Normal Hours	40	20	20	385
4	Hours Worked	40	0	0	346
5	Tax Code	300L	300L	300L	

3. To re-display column **K**, highlight a range in column **J** to column **L**, e.g. **J1:L1** and click the **Format** button, select **Hide and Unhide** and click **Unhide Columns**.

4. A row can be hidden in a similar way, but another method is to use the shortcut menu. Right click on the row heading **2** and select **Hide**.

5. To re-display row **2**, select rows **1** to **3**, in the row headings, right click and select **Unhide**.

6. Columns/Rows may also be hidden by dragging their borders until the column width or the row height is zero. Using this method to hide column **M**, place the mouse pointer on the column divider between **N** and **M**. Drag the adjust cursor to the left, carefully, till the column width is **0.00**.

Note: *Dragging further left hides multiple columns. If this happens, use **Undo** to restore the columns and try again.*

7. The mouse can also be used to unhide columns or rows. There are two adjust cursors, displayed in the row and column headings. The normal column adjust cursor is on the left and for a row is above. To the right of a hidden column or below a hidden row the adjust cursor changes to ‖ or ‗. Dragging this cursor redisplays the hidden data. Unhide column **M** making it **10.00** units wide.

8. Close the workbook <u>without</u> saving.

Exercise 51 - Revision

1. Open the workbook **Savings**.

2. Enter various amounts for **Extra** income across row **3** between **100** and **200**.

3. **Right** align the labels in the range **B1:N1**.

4. Replace **Rent** with **Mortgage** in cell **A5**. Your **Mortgage** is **565** per month add this to row **5**.

5. Two items of expenditure have been omitted: **Electricity** and **Gas**. Highlight rows **9** and **10** using the row numbers, right click and select **Insert**, to add two new rows. Enter the two labels.

6. Drag the formula from **N8** down to **N9** and **N10**.

7. **Leisure** and **Holidays** are similar. Delete row **6** by right clicking on the row number and selecting **Delete**.

8. Widen column **A** to **90 pixels**. Edit the label in **A3** to **Extra Income** and **Income** in **A4** to **Total Income**.

9. Reduce columns **B** through to **M** to **60 pixels** wide.

10. Add numbers to the **Expenses** block, rows **6** to **13**.

11. In cell **B15** enter the formula to calculate the savings for January, **Total Income - Expenses**.

12. In cell **C15** the **Savings** are going to accumulate, enter the formula **=B15+C4-C14**

13. Copy the formula across the row using the **Fill Handle** to cell **M15**. In cell **N15** the formula is simply **=M15**, the previous cell.

14. **Print Preview** the worksheet. There are two pages.

15. Change the paper **Orientation** to **Landscape** and then print one copy of the worksheet.

16. Save the workbook as **Savings2** and close the workbook.

Section 8

Creating Charts

By the end of this Section you should be able to:

Create a Quick Chart

Understand the Different Chart Types

Choose an Appropriate Data Source

Use Different Chart Types

Create Comparative Charts

Exercise 52 - Quick Chart

Guidelines:

The quickest way to create a basic column chart is to highlight the required range and press the function key <**F11**>. The chart is created and placed on a separate sheet, called **Chart1**.

The **Charts** group on the **Insert** tab allows you to select the chart type to be inserted. This is covered in the next few exercises.

Actions:

1.   Open the workbook **Teamdata**.

2.   Highlight the cell range **A3:B11** and press the function key <**F11**>.

3.   A basic column chart is created on a **Chart1** worksheet.

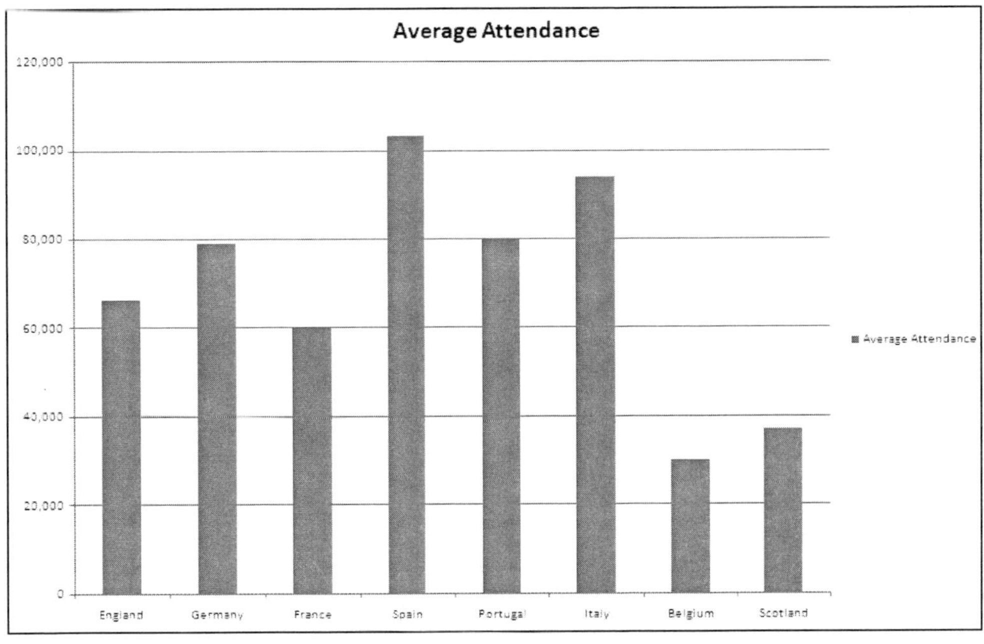

4.   Leave the workbook open for the next exercise.

Exercise 53 - Chart Types

Guidelines:

There are different charts available to display different types of information. The most popular and common chart types include:

Column	Shaded vertical columns, compares values across categories, often shows quantity values, e.g. rainfall for August, sales for 2001.
Line	Points connected by a line, shows discrete values, e.g. share price at close of trading each day, temperature reading every hour, often displays a trend over time or categories
Pie	Data as slices of circular pie, displays the contribution of each value to a total
Bar	Shaded horizontal bars, compares values across categories
Area	Similar to a line chart but where the area below the line is coloured.
Scatter	Unconnected points, usually used when both the X and Y axis are measured values with uneven intervals, e.g. scientific data.
Other Charts	Include Stock, Surface and Doughnut, Bubble, Radar charts.
Combination	One chart with two series displayed using two different chart types, e.g. a chart with one series shown as columns and one as a line.

There are also variations of these charts available, e.g. 3-D charts.

Actions:

1. With the workbook **Teamdata** open, click the **teamdata** tab to display the data.

2. With the range **A3:B11** highlighted, display the **Insert** tab, in the **Chart** group, click the **Column** button to display a list of available **Column Charts**.

3. Click each button in the **Charts** group in turn to see the available charts in each group.

*Note: Each menu has an **All Chart Types** option. This displays the **Insert Chart** dialog box where all chart types are displayed.*

4. Close the workbook <u>without</u> saving.

Exercise 54 - Column Charts

Guidelines:

Column Charts represent category data as vertically shaded columns and are the most commonly used charts.

Actions:

1. Open the file **cinedata.csv**. If the file is not shown, select **All Files** from the box to the right of the **File name** box.

2. Save this file as a **Excel Workbook** (**xlsx** format), keeping the same name.

3. Make sure all of the data is visible by widening the columns if necessary.

4. Highlight the range **A3:B10** to begin charting the audience figures in Newcastle.

	A	B	C	D	E	F
1	Cinema Audiences					
2						
3	Audiences	Newcastle	Birmingham	Glasgow	Total	
4	Monday	500	600	575	1675	
5	Tuesday	800	625	1750	3175	
6	Wednesday	750	750	800	2300	
7	Thursday	2000	675	850	3525	
8	Friday	3000	2750	3100	8850	
9	Saturday	3125	3300	3325	9750	
10	Sunday	525	2000	300	2825	
11	Totals	10700	10700	10700	32100	
12						

Note: Selecting the titles in row **3** and column **A** will later automatically add the **Chart Title** and **Legend** as **Newcastle** and the days as the **Horizontal Axis** labels.

5. Click the **Column** chart button, , on the **Insert** tab.

continued over

Exercise 54 - Continued

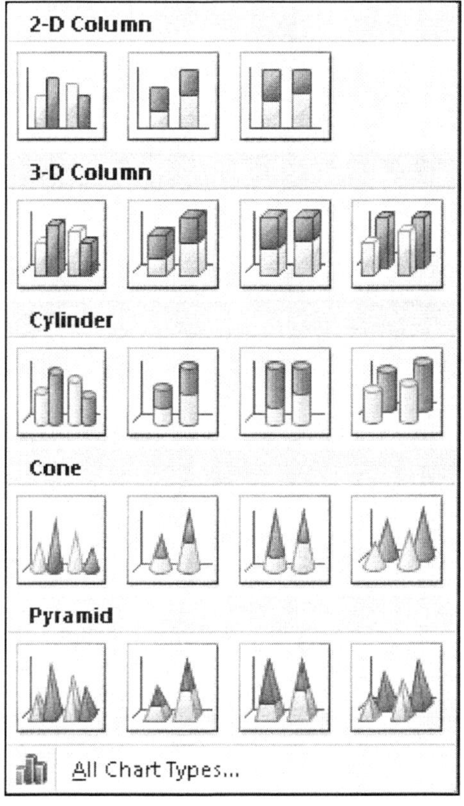

6.   Click **Clustered Column** under **2-D Column** from the list.

7.   The chart is created and placed on the worksheet with the data.

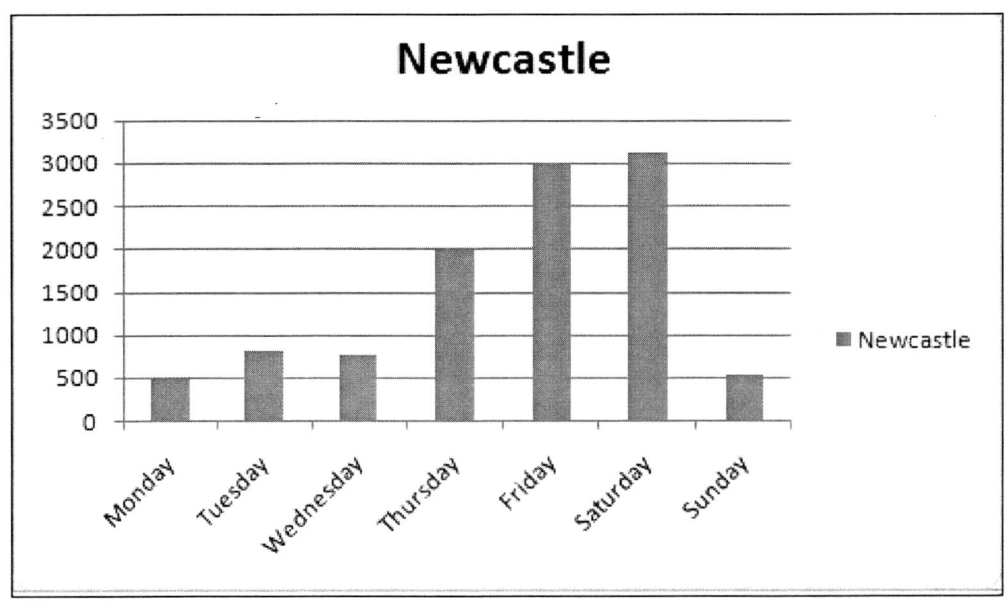

continued over

Exercise 54 - Continued

8. Click on the chart to make sure that it is selected, then click the **Move Chart** button in the **Location** group. Select **New Sheet** from the **Move Chart** dialog box.

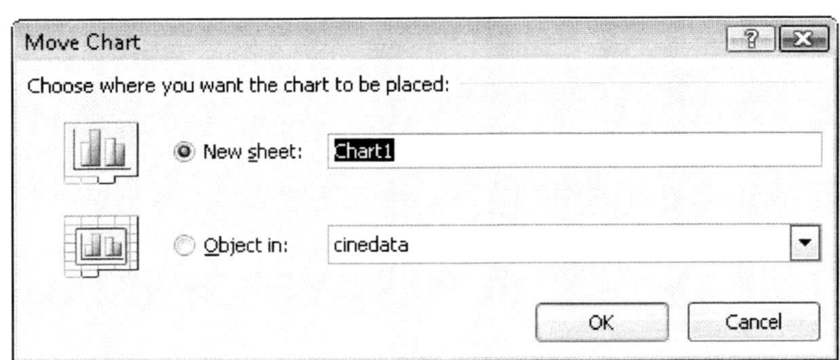

9. Click **OK.** The chart is now displayed on a new sheet.

10. The chart is showing the legend **Newcastle**

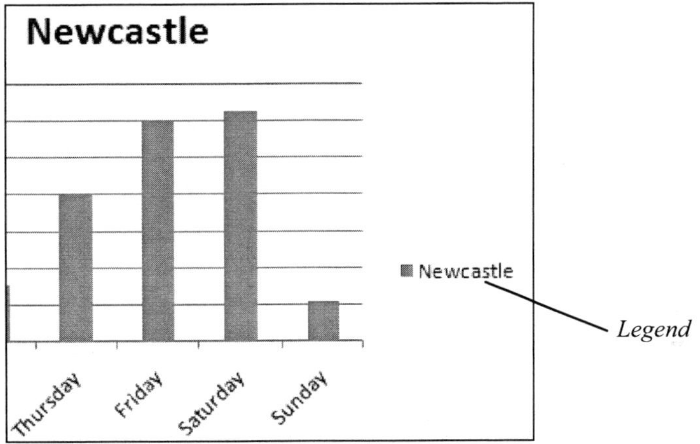

11. Right click on the **legend** Newcastle and select **Delete**.

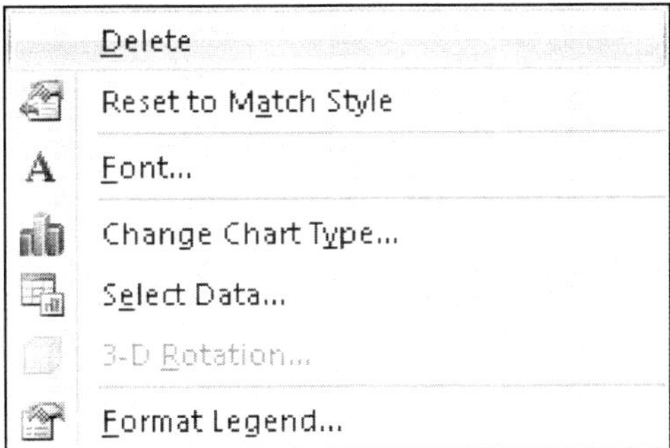

12. Save the workbook as **cinedata2**.

13. Close the workbook.

Exercise 55 - Bar Charts

Guidelines:

Bar charts are similar to **Column charts** except that the data is displayed as horizontal bars. The two axes are changed round with the category axis vertical and the value axis horizontal.

Actions:

1. Start a new workbook and create the worksheet as shown below.

	A	B	C
1	WORLD POPULATION (Millions)		
2			
3	Region	Population	
4	Asia	495	
5	Africa	448	
6	North America	265	
7	South America	289	
8	Europe	642	
9	CIS	278	
10	World	2417	
11			

These figures are not an accurate representation of the world's population

2. Widen column **A** by positioning the mouse pointer between the column **A** and **B** headings until it changes to a ✛, then click and drag the pointer to the right until the column is wide enough to display all of the text.

3. Select the data to be used by highlighting the range, **A3:B9**.

	A	B	C
1	WORLD POPULATION (Millions)		
2			
3	Region	Population	
4	Asia	495	
5	Africa	448	
6	North America	265	
7	South America	289	
8	Europe	642	
9	CIS	278	
10	World	2417	
11			

4. Click the **Bar** button in the **Charts** group.

continued over

Exercise 55 - Continued

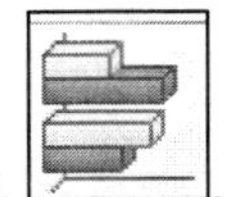

5.   Select **Clustered Bar in 3-D**, .

6.   To add a label to the chart, click the **Axis Titles** button on the **Layout** tab. Select **Primary Horizontal Axis Title** and **Title Below Axis**.

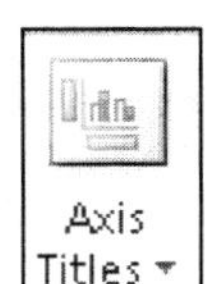

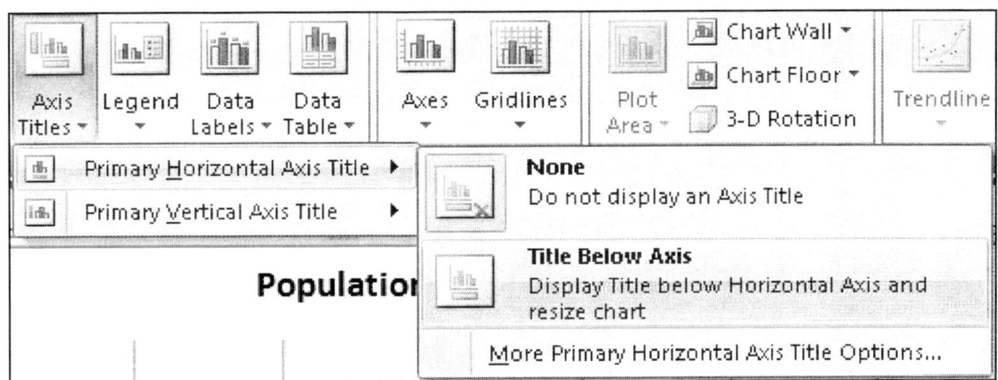

7.   Type **Population in Millions** and press <**Enter**> to add the axis title.

8.   To add the vertical axis title, click **Axis Titles** and select **Primary Vertical Axis Title,** then **Rotated Title** and enter the title **Regions**.

9.   Remove the **Legend**.

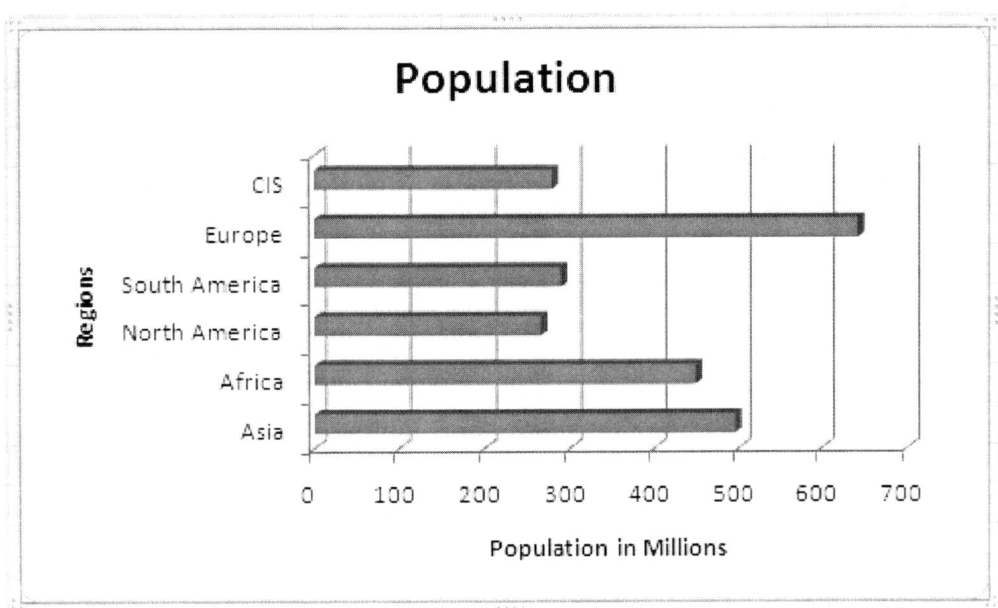

10.   Save the workbook as **Population** and then close it.

Exercise 56 - Pie Charts

Guidelines:

A pie chart shows data as slices of pie. The size of each piece of pie represents the value of the data on which it is based, as a fraction of the total. When all pieces are added together, they show the sum of the original data, as a complete circle (pie).

Actions:

1.   Open the workbook **compdata.csv**.

2.   Save the file as a **Excel Workbook** (**xlsx** format), keeping the same name.

3.   Make sure all of the data can be seen, widening the columns if necessary.

4.   Highlight the data in the cells **A1:B6** (totals are rarely included in charts), display the **Insert** tab and click the **Pie** chart button.

5.   From the **Chart sub-type** area, choose the second option from the first row, **Exploded Pie**. An exploded pie chart, can be used to emphasise a particular piece of data (see step 10).

6.   The exploded pie chart is now shown.

Note: ***Legends*** *and* ***Data Labels*** *can also be changed, as described in later exercises.*

7.   Which town has the lowest computer sales (the smallest slice of pie)? (The answer is listed in the **Answer Section** at the end of the guide).

8.   Click once on this 'slice of pie' to select all of the slices, then click again to highlight this slice only.

9.   Click and drag the smallest slice outwards, so it stands out from the rest of the chart.

10.   Save the workbook as **compdata2** and close it.

Exercise 57 - Line Charts

Guidelines:

A line chart is used to show trends in data at equal intervals.

Actions:

1. Open the workbook **Cashflow**.

2. The source data so far has been in one block, data that is not together can also be charted. To select non-adjacent data, highlight the data in the cells **A1:M1** (the months, used for the labels), hold down <Ctrl> and highlight the range **A11:M11** (the profit values from January to December). Release the mouse button and then release <Ctrl>. The two ranges are now selected.

3. Click the **Insert** tab and select **Line** chart, 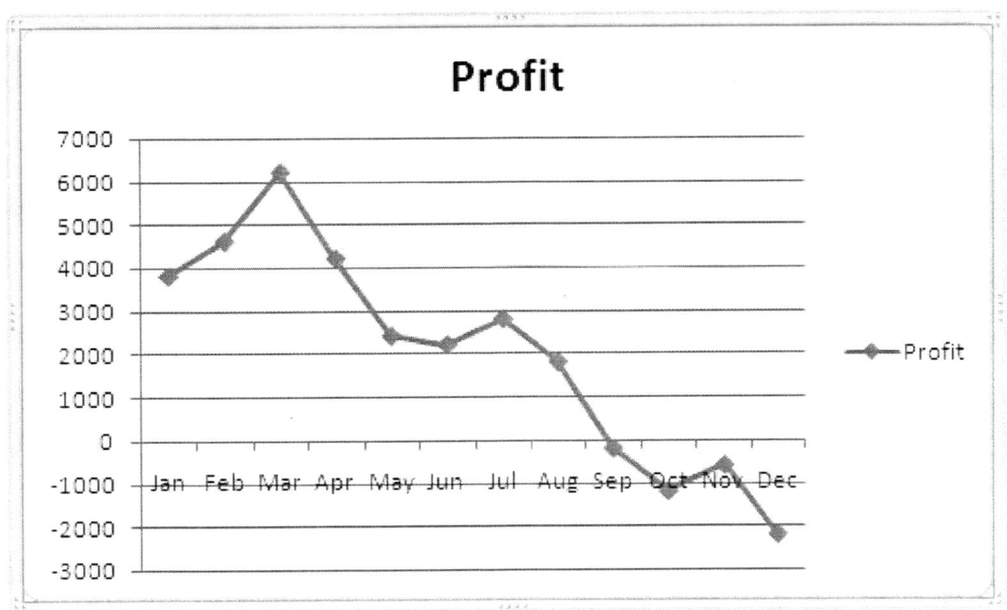. Select **Line with markers**.

3. Click the **Insert** tab and select **Line** chart. Select **Line with markers**.

4. The line chart is now displayed with the data.

5. On the **Design** tab, click **Move Chart**, select the **New sheet** option and click **OK** to move the chart to a separate sheet, named **Chart1**.

6. Which month has the highest profit (the answer is listed in the **Answer Section** at the end of the guide)?

7. Save the workbook as **Cashflow2** and close it.

Exercise 58 - Comparative Charts

Guidelines:

More than one data set can be represented on one chart to show a comparison between the data. This type of chart displays either the data as two columns, two lines, or one data set as columns and another set as a line. To create comparison charts of two columns or two lines, the data is selected and charts are created in the same way as previously covered.

For two sets of related data (sharing the same axis) the type is a **Line - Column** chart. This type of chart can also be used to represent two sets of unrelated data, e.g. rainfall as columns and temperature as a line but the type is then **Line - Column on 2 Axes**.

Actions:

1. Open **Rainfall**. This spreadsheet shows the daily rainfall in July for the cities of London and Bombay, and it shows the average daily rainfall for these cities in this month.

2. To plot a chart of London's daily rainfall against London's average rainfall, highlight cells **A4:B19** (labels to be used and London's daily rainfall). Hold down <Ctrl> and select the second range **D4:D19**.

3. Once the required data ranges are selected, click the **Insert** tab, and select the **Column** button. Create a **2-D Clustered Column** chart.

4. Highlight the **London Average** bars by clicking on one of the red columns in the chart.

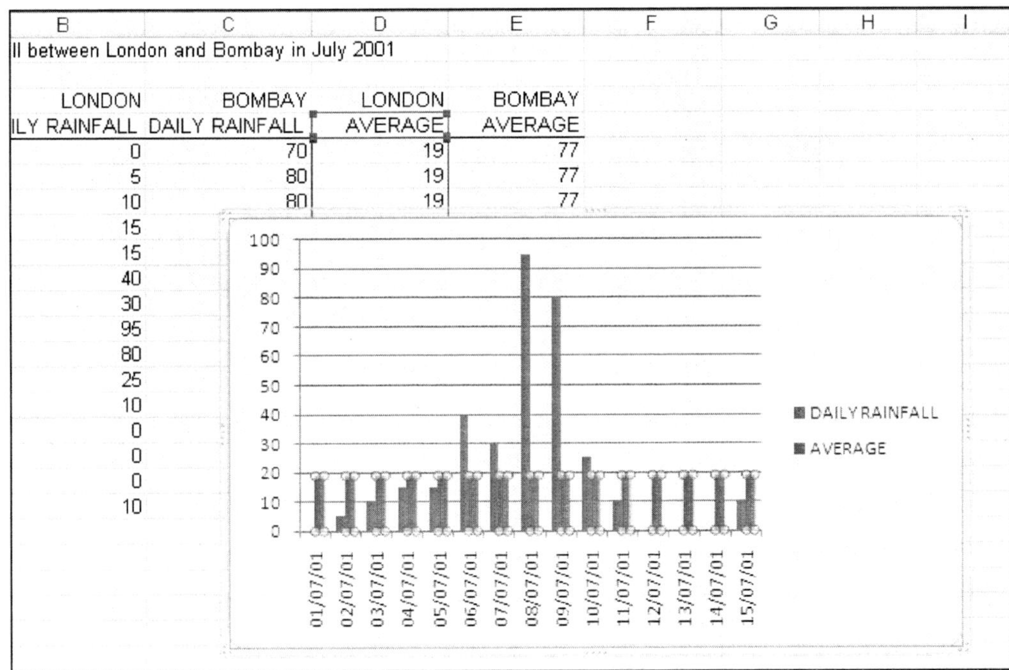

continued over

Exercise 58 - Continued

5.   Right click and select **Change Series Chart Type**.

6.   Click **Line** and select **OK.**

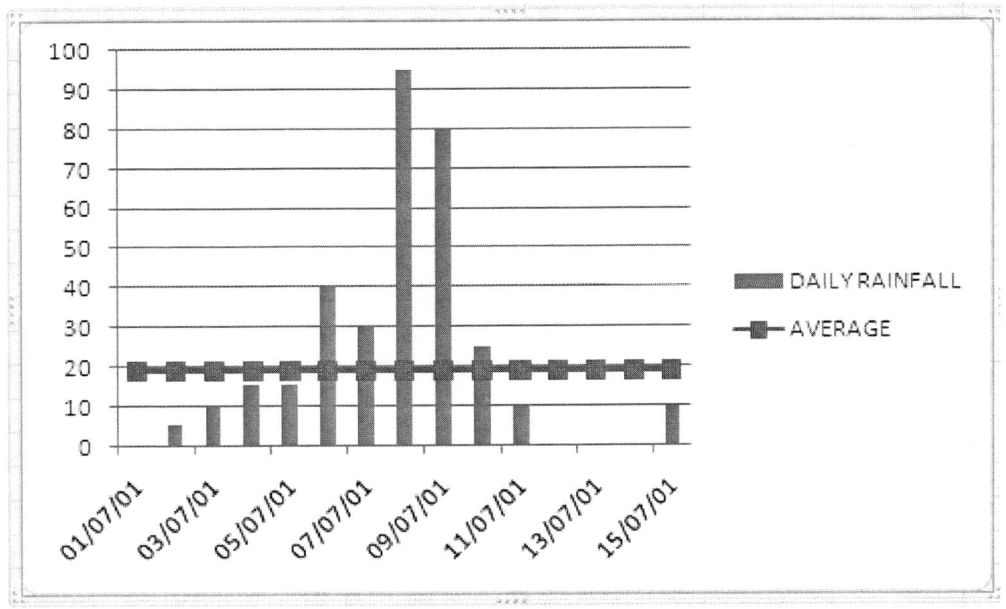

7.   Display the **Layout** tab and click the **Chart Title** button and select **Above Chart** to add a chart title **Rainfall in London July 2001**.

8.   Add a **Vertical Axis Title** as **Rainfall (mm)**, as rotated text.

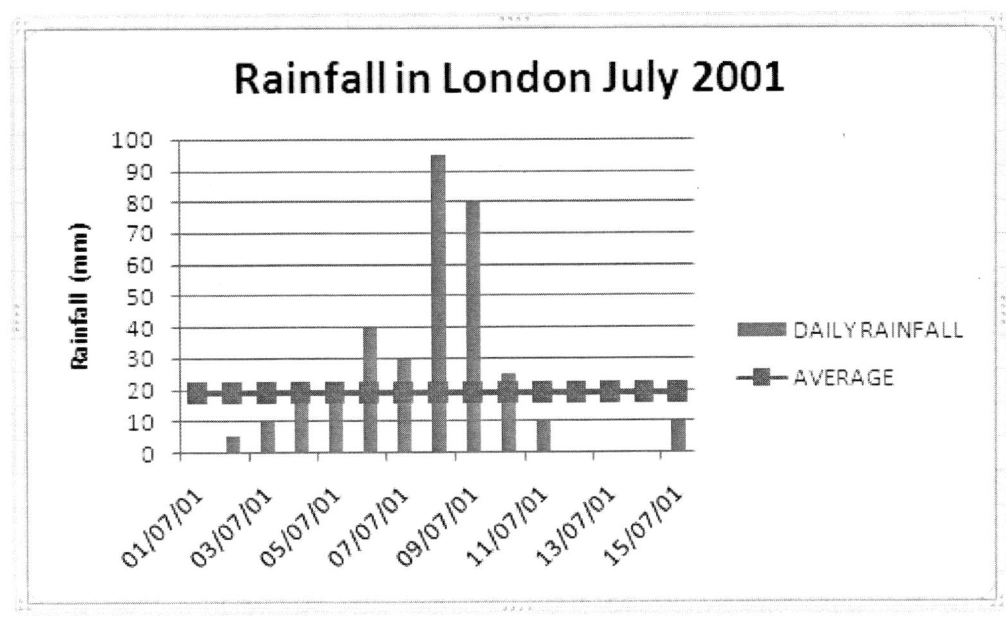

9.   Save the workbook as **Rainfall2** and close it.

          © CiA Training Ltd 2007

Exercise 59 - Scatter Charts

Guidelines:

When both axes of a chart are based on variables, such as plotting **Height** against **Weight** for a sample of people, it is necessary to use a **Scatter Chart** to try and establish whether there is a relationship between the two variables. Scatter charts can also be useful to identify trends from plotted data.

Actions:

1. Open the workbook **Scatter**. This spreadsheet shows the amount of rainfall taken in a random sample.

2. With the cursor in cell **A1** display the **Insert** tab and click the **Scatter** button and select the **Scatter with only Markers** graph. The data is selected automatically.

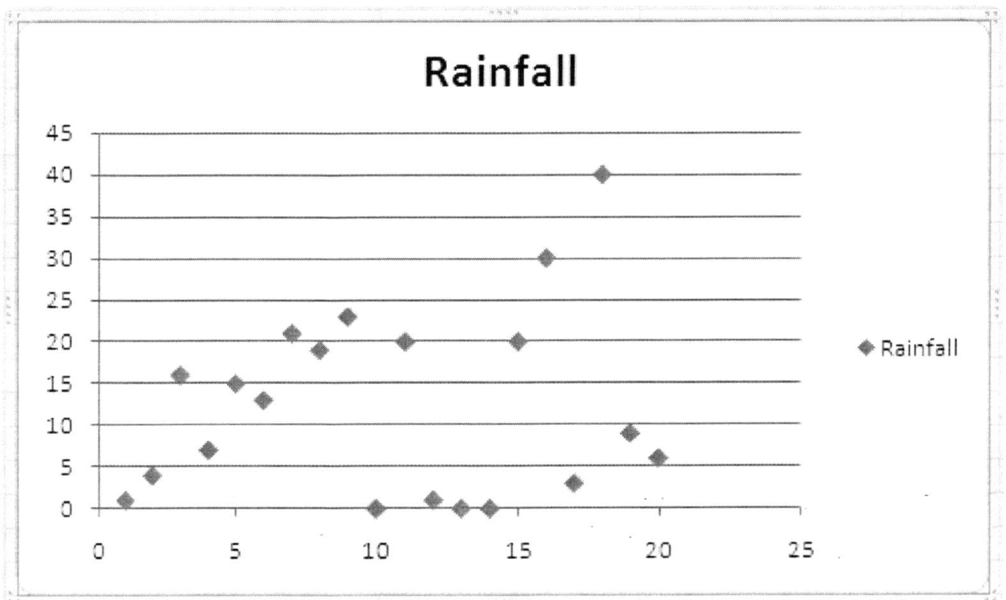

3. Click on the **Chart Title** and change the text to **Precipitation Measurements**, by selecting and overtyping.

4. Add **Sample** as the **Horizontal Axis Title**.

5. Add **Rainfall (mm)** as the **Vertical Axis Title**, as rotated text.

6. Remove the **Legend**.

7. Save the workbook as **Scatter2** (the completed chart is listed in the **Answer Section** at the end of the guide).

8. Close the workbook.

Exercise 60 - Revision

1. What key can be is used to create a chart in **Excel**?

2. How is this feature started?

3. Would you select the source data before or after starting to create a chart? Why?

4. Name the three most commonly used types of chart.

5. Name the other chart types.

6. Which chart is best at showing trends?

7. Which chart displays data that appears to be totally random?

8. If you were given the weekly sales figures for a company, what type of chart would you create to best demonstrate the data?

9. What type of chart would you create to represent the data obtained from a scientific experiment with two variables?

10. What type of chart would you create to represent the breakdown of costs involved with producing a particular product?

11. A **Bar Chart** and a **Column Chart** are similar, but what is the difference?

Note: *The answers are listed in the **Answer Section** at the end of the guide.*

Section 9

Setting Chart Parameters

By the end of this Section you should be able to:

Add and Format Titles

Add Data Labels

Add and Remove Legends

Change Intervals and Limits on Axis

Insert Text Boxes

Exercise 61 - Titles

Guidelines:

Chart and **Axis Titles** are used to show the measurements used and help show what the chart represents. Once a chart has been produced, the titles can be modified and formatted as required.

Actions:

1. Open the file **cinedata2.xls** (created and saved in **Exercise 54**).

2. Click on the **Chart1** tab at the bottom of the screen to see the first chart created.

3. The title of the chart is to be amended and formatted. Click once on the **Newcastle** title and click again to place the cursor within the text.

4. Press <**Home**> to move the cursor to the start of the title text and type **Audiences in** followed by a space. Press <**End**> to move the cursor to the end of the text. Press <**Enter**> to create a second line. Type **Week 27 in 2005**.

5. Select all the text in the title.

6. Move the cursor up slightly and the shortcut formatting menu is displayed. The title is already **Bold** and font size **18**.

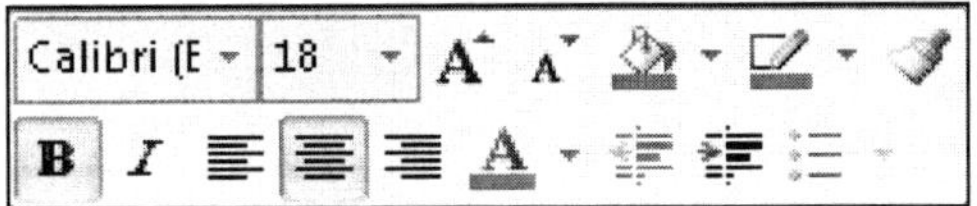

7. Select **Italic** and **24** from the **Size** box.

8. Click on the **Format** tab and try the different **WordArt Styles** and **Shape Styles** to change the styling of the title.

9. Add a **Horizontal Axis Title** as **Days of the Week**, using the **Layout** tab.

10. Add a **Vertical Axis Title**, rotated text as **Number of People**.

11. The **Horizontal Axis Title** is not necessary, so is to be deleted, Click on **Days of the Week** once to select it and press <**Delete**>.

12. Save the workbook using the same name and leave it open.

Exercise 62 - Data Labels

Guidelines:

Data labels are the actual values of the individual data points. When added to a chart they make it easier to interpret.

Actions:

1. The workbook **cinedata2** should still be open, if not, open it.

2. If it is not displayed, click on the **Chart1** sheet to display the first chart created.

3. Display the **Layout** tab and select the **Data Labels** button in the **Labels** group.

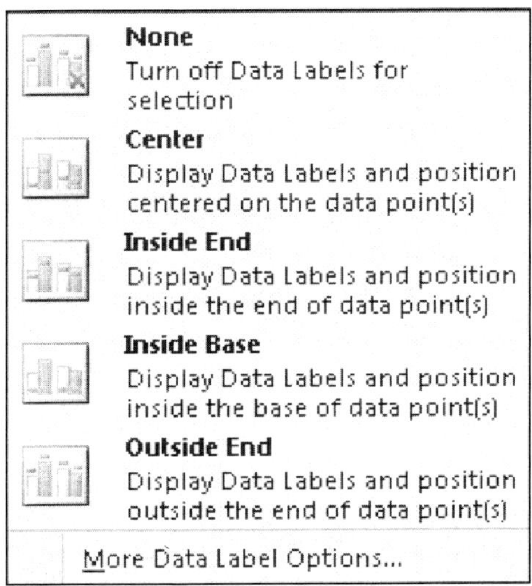

4. There are six available options. The options allow you to change the way the labels are displayed on the chart. Select **Inside End**.

5. Data label settings for a **Pie Chart** offer different options. Ensure that the chart on the **Chart1** sheet is selected. Right click the chart and select **Change Chart Type**.

6. Click on **Pie** in the **Change Chart type**: list and then click **OK**. The original **Column Chart** has been changed into a **Pie Chart**, still with the same data labels displayed.

7. With the **Pie Chart** active, right click and select **Format Data Labels**.

continued over

Exercise 62 - Continued

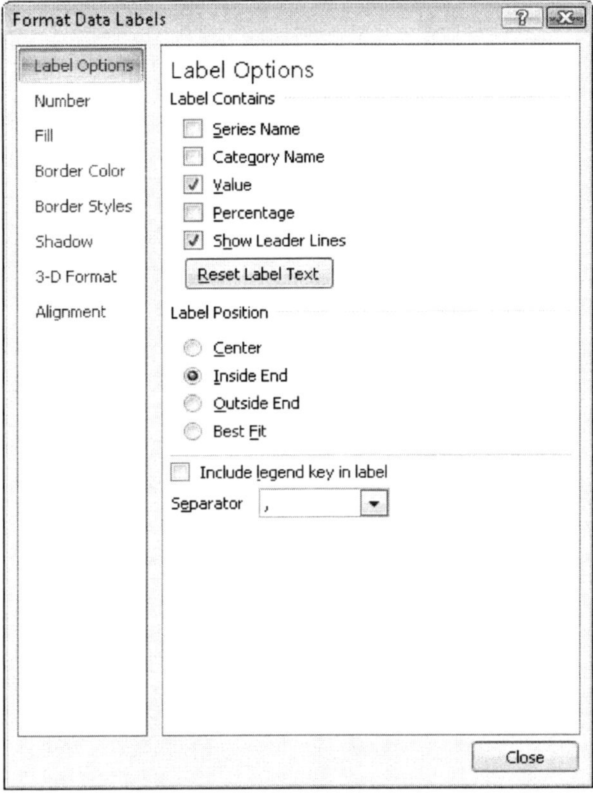

8. Note that the **Value** option is already selected, uncheck **Value**. Check **Percentage** and **Category Name** and then click **Close** to display the pie chart showing the name of each segment, together with its size as a percentage of the whole sample.

9. To show the labels on the outside of the pie chart next to each segment click **Data Labels** and select **Outside End**.

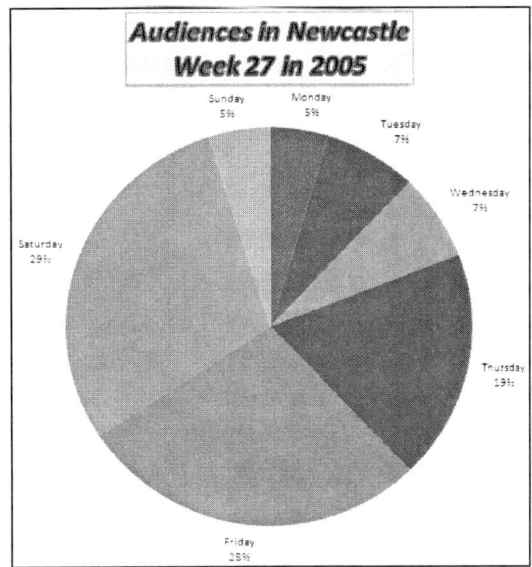

10. Save the workbook as **cinedata3** and then close it.

Exercise 63 - Legends

Guidelines:

A legend is a box that identifies the patterns or colours assigned to the data series or categories in a chart. It is primarily used to show the identity of each data series when more than one set of data is being displayed.

Note: *To create a **Legend** when selecting the data, highlight the titles of the data being displayed. These will automatically be shown as the **Legend**.*

Actions:

1. Open the workbook **Cashflow2** (saved in **Exercise 57**) and click on the **Chart1** sheet tab to view the chart.

2. The legend can easily be removed from the chart, as it is not needed. Click once on the legend to select it.

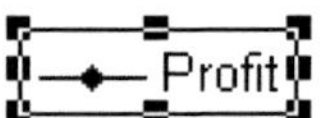

3. Press <**Delete**> or click the **Legend** button from the **Layout** tab and select **None.**

4. To add a legend to the chart again, with the chart active, click the **Layout** tab and select the **Legend** button.

5. Select **Show Legend at Bottom**.

6. Click on the legend to select it, hold the mouse button down and drag the legend to the top right corner.

7. Close the workbook <u>without</u> saving any changes.

Exercise 64 - Set Limits and Intervals on Axes

Guidelines:

When displaying charts, they appear easier to understand and look more presentable if the value axis uses an appropriate scale. This may involve changing the lower value of the axis, normally the **Minimum** is set to **0**. The **Maximum** can also be changed, if necessary.

Actions:

1.   Open the workbook **Houses** and display the **Houses** sheet.

2.   The values on the chart are all large numbers and the axis has no values between 0 to 60,000 or over 100,000. Therefore the axis can be edited to change the range of values it displays.

3.   Right click anywhere on the **Average Price (£)** axis and select the **Format Axis** dialog box.

4.   Both the minimum and maximum limits can be changed in this dialog box. Enter **60000** as the **Minimum**.

5.   Enter **100000** as the **Maximum**.

6.   Enter the **Major unit** (the axis interval) **Fixed** to **10000**.

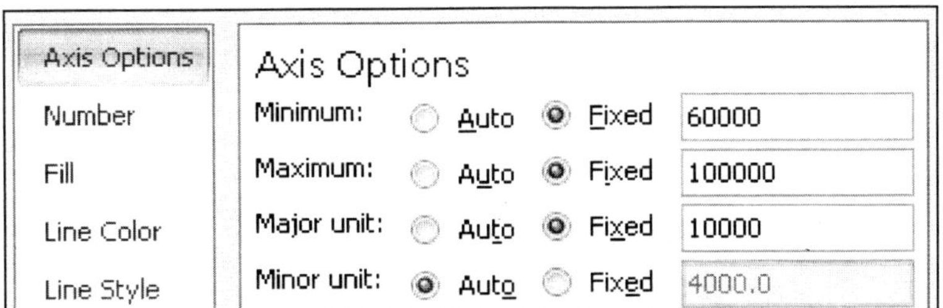

7.   Click **Close**. The dialog box closes and the chart appears with a more suitable scale.

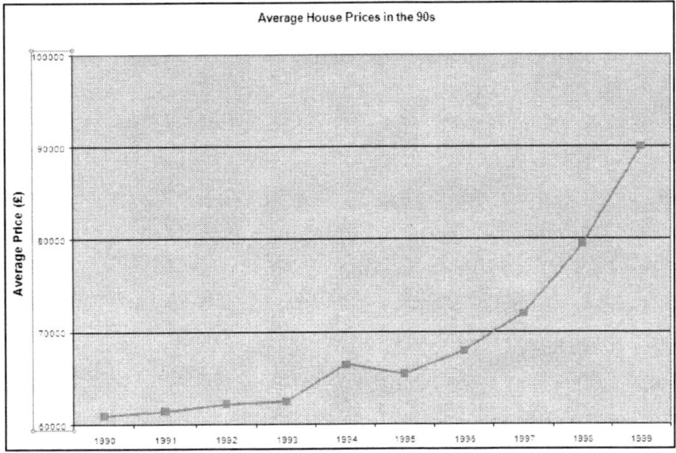

8.   Save the workbook as **Houses2** and close it.

Exercise 65 - Text Boxes

Guidelines:

A **Text Box** is a way of adding unattached supporting text to describe part of a chart. Text boxes can be placed anywhere on a chart and be of any size.

Actions:

1. Open the workbook **Rainfall2** (created in **Exercise 58**). Right click and **Move Chart**. Select **New sheet** and click **OK**.

2. Text boxes are to be added to show which area is below, and which area is above average rainfall. The **Layout** tab must be displayed. The **Text Box** button is shown on the **Insert** group.

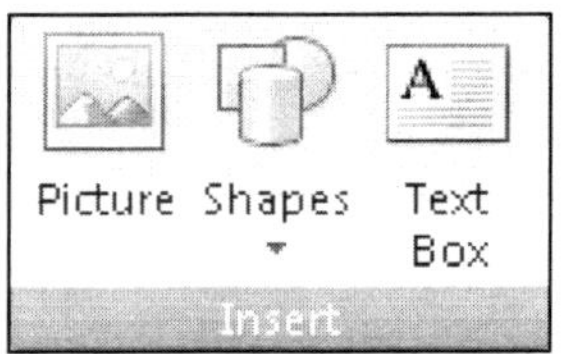

3. Click the **Text Box** button, in the **Insert** group.

4. Click and drag a small box on the chart below the average line as shown below. When the mouse is released, the text box appears.

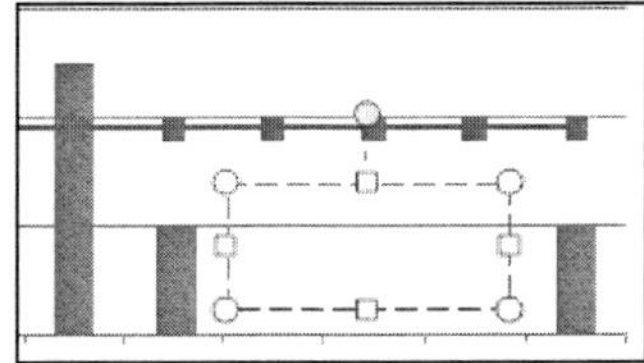

5. Type **Below Average** in the box and click away from the box to complete the entry.

6. Create another text box above the line containing the text **Above Average**.

7. To make the border of the text box visible, right click on one of the text boxes and select **Format Shape** to add a border, using **Line Color** and the **Solid line** options.

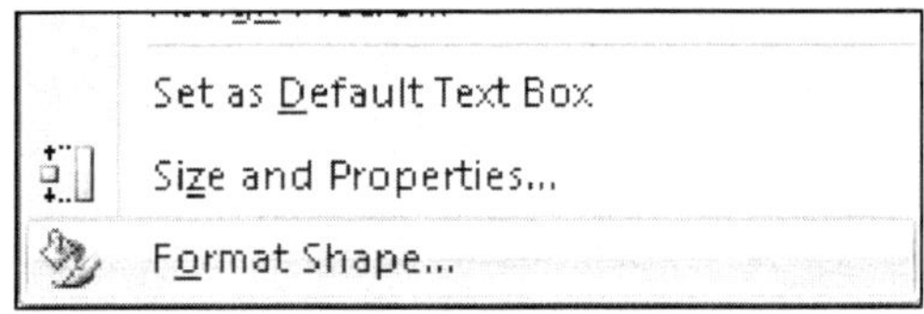

8. Save the workbook using the same name.

9. Close the workbook.

Exercise 66 - Revision

1. Open the workbook **Teamdata**.

2. Create a **Bar Chart** of the data range **A3:B11**, with the **Horizontal Axis Title** as **Attendance**, the **Vertical Axis Title** as **Country** and place on a new sheet called **Bar Chart**.

3. Change the main title to **Average Football** with **Attendance** as a second line. Add a border and change the font size to **24pt**.

4. Change the lower limit on the **Horizontal (Value) axis** to **20000**.

5. Remove the **Legend**.

6. Display the values on outside end of the bars.

7. Create a **Text Box** away from the bars in the top right of the **Plot Area** with the text **Home Games Only**. Increase the font size to **12pt** and add a border.

8. Save the file as a workbook named **Football**.

9. Close the workbook.

*Note: The completed chart is listed in the **Answer Section** at the end of the guide).*

Exercise 67 - Revision

1. Open the workbook **Company**.

2. Highlight the range **A1:M2** and press **<F11>** to create a chart.

3. Display the chart and change the minimum value to **2500** on the vertical axis.

4. Change the chart title to **Product Sales**. Format the chart title appropriately to make it stand out.

5. Add a **Text Box** to the top right of the plot area with the text **These sales are pathetic!** Format the text appropriately.

6. Save the workbook as **Company3**.

7. Close the workbook.

*Note: A sample solution is listed in the **Answer Section** at the end of the guide.*

Section 10

Formatting Charts

By the end of this Section you should be able to:

Apply Numeric Formatting on Axes

Apply Fill Colour to the Data Series

Exercise 68 - Numbers on Axes

Guidelines:

The numbers on the **Vertical (Category) Axis** can be formatted as required, i.e. as numbers, numbers with decimal places, dates or percentages in exactly the same way as all numbers in *Excel*. The orientation of the labels can be rotated at any angle. Rotated ninety degrees to make the labels easier to read is the most common format.

Actions:

1. Open the workbook **Cashflow2**, saved in **Exercise 57**.

2. Using the chart on the **Chart1** sheet, right click on the **Vertical (Category) Axis** and select **Format Axis** to display the **Format Axis** dialog box.

3. Select the **Number** option.

4. Select **Currency** from the list and choose the second or fourth option from the **Negative numbers** section, so all negative numbers appear **red**, with, or without a minus sign.

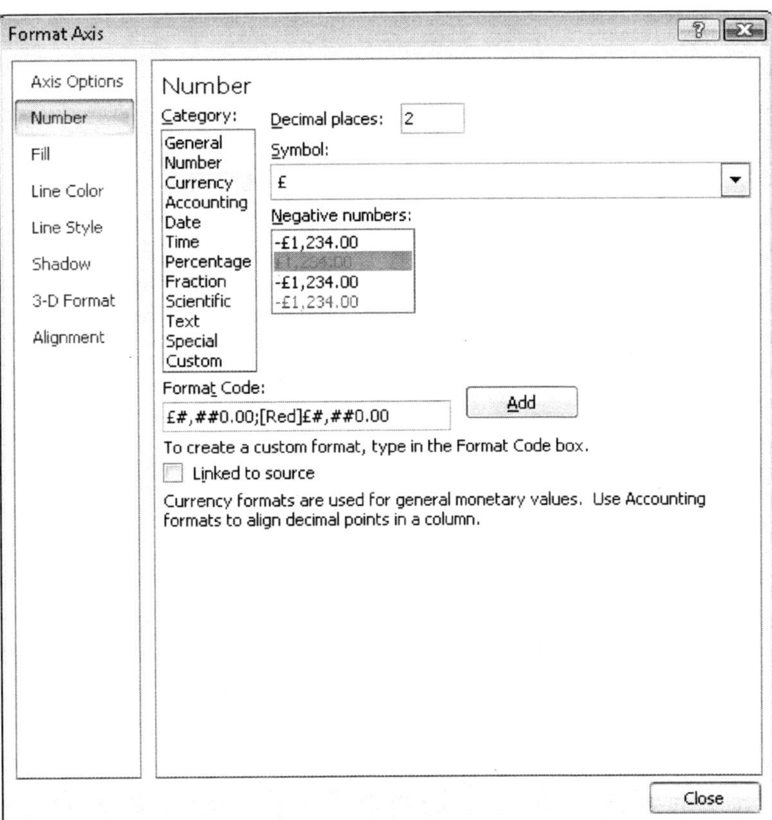

5. Leave the **Decimal places** as **2** and click **Close** to apply the changes.

continued over

Exercise 68 - Continued

6. Save the workbook using same name and close it.

7. Open the **Rainfall2** workbook and view **Chart1**.

8. To make the dates easier to read, right click on any date and display the **Format Axis** dialog box.

9. Select **Alignment** and from the **Text direction** drop down select **Rotate all text 270°**.

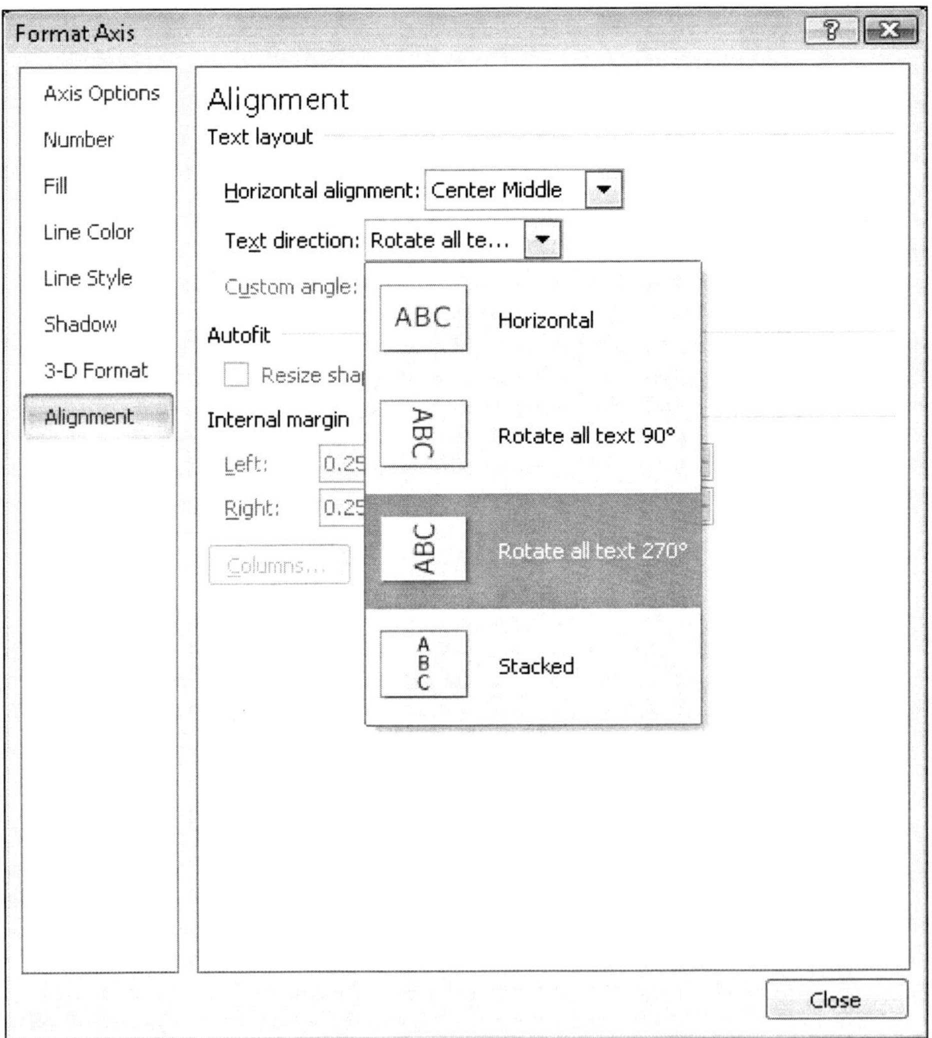

10. Click **Close** to see the effect.

11. Right click any date again, select **Format Axis**, and from the **Number** section, choose **Date** from the **Category** list and then the **dd/mm/yyyy** from the **Type** list. Click **Close** to see the date change formats.

12. Save the workbook using the same name and close it.

Exercise 69 - Data Series Colour

Guidelines:

With a bar, column or pie chart, the data series can be filled with any colour or any pattern. Different patterns (various types of shading) are used when a colour printer is not available or to display comparative data series.

Actions:

1. Open the workbook **Hydrogen** and display the chart on the **Hydrogen** sheet tab.

2. To change all of the columns to a different colour, double click on any column to display the **Design** tab.

3. Click the **More** button at the right end of the **Chart Styles** group. Choose a different colour.

4. Save the workbook as **Hydrogen2** and close it.

5. Open the workbook **cinedata2** (saved in **Exercise 54**) and display **Chart1**.

6. Click on any of the **Newcastle** columns, display the **Format** tab and then click the **Shape Fill** button.

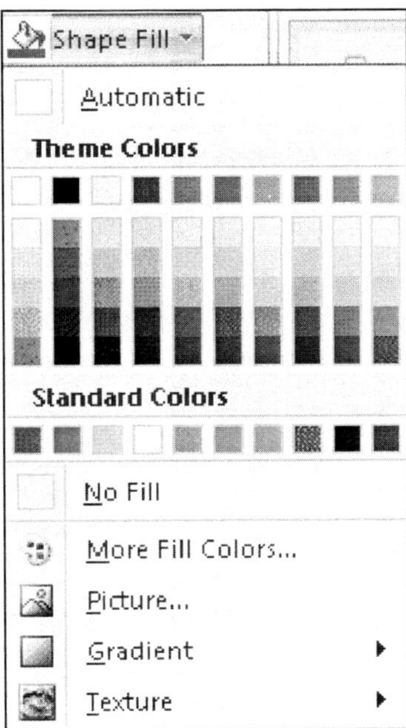

7. Choose a suitable colour and make a selection from within **Shape Effects**.

8. Save the workbook using the same name and close it.

Note: *A sample finished chart can be seen within **Answer Section** at the end of the guide.*

Exercise 70 - Revision

1. Open the workbook **Cashflow2** (this workbook includes a line chart and was developed and saved from **Cashflow** in **Exercise 57**).

2. Display the **Chart1** sheet tab, if not displayed.

3. Apply the following styles:

    Chart title   font size **24**, **italic**

    Legend   font size **12**

4. Format the data series line to be dotted.

5. Save the workbook as **Cashflow3**.

6. Close the workbook.

Exercise 71 - Revision

1. Open the workbook **cinedata.csv**.

2. Create a column chart on a new sheet to display the audiences in **Glasgow**. Add the chart title **Glasgow Audiences** and suitable axes titles.

3. Change the colour of the columns.

4. Format the chart title text to be **italic** and size **20pt**.

5. To the chart title box, add a light grey background with a border and a shadow effect.

6. Remove the legend.

7. Save the file as a workbook, as **Audiences**.

8. Close the workbook.

*Note: The completed chart is listed in the **Answer Section** at the back of the guide.*

Section 11

Printing Charts

By the end of this Section you should be able to:

Print Charts

Change Chart Orientation

Exercise 72 - Printing Charts

Guidelines:

The **Print** command controls what is printed, how it is printed and number of copies, etc.

Actions:

1. Open the workbook **Cinemadata** and display **Chart1** on screen.

2. Select the **Office Button** and click **Print** to display the **Print** dialog box.

3. Click **OK** to print with the default settings, i.e. one copy of the active worksheet. The **Print range** and **Print what** options are not covered in this guide.

4. Display the **Cinema Data** sheet. This sheet contains the data and an embedded chart (a chart created on the same sheet as the data). This chart shows the audiences for **Birmingham**.

5. To print the data and the chart, click on any cell in the sheet and print using the **Office Button,** place the cursor over **Print** to display the print options on the right and click **Quick Print**. A single copy of the worksheet is printed without displaying the **Print** dialog box.

6. To print an embedded chart without the data, click on the chart to make it active and then select the **Office Button** and select **Print**.

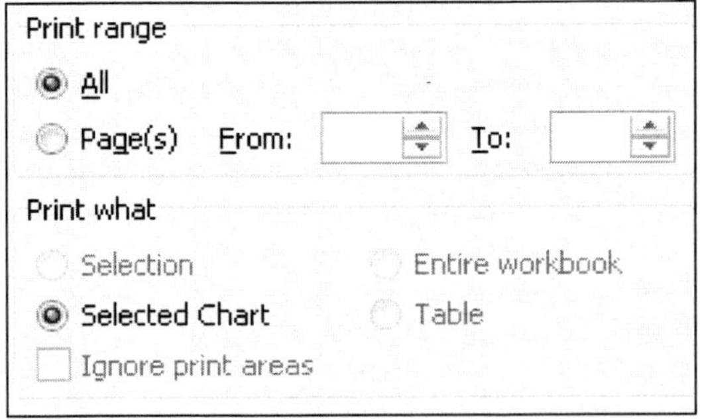

7. Under **Print what** the **Selected Chart** option is displayed, automatically. Click **OK** to print the chart on a full sheet. As this option is selected by default the **Quick Print** option could have been used to achieve the same effect.

8. Compare the quality of the two printouts. A chart created on its own sheet is of a higher quality.

9. Leave the workbook open for the next exercise.

Exercise 73 - Chart Orientation

Guidelines:

Orientation is the way the chart is placed on the paper, either **Landscape** - horizontal (the default for charts) or **Portrait** - vertical (the default for standard worksheets). The **Orientation** is changed using the **Orientation** button on the **Page Layout** tab in the **Page Setup** group.

Actions:

1. The workbook **Cinemadata** should still be open from the previous exercise, if not, open it.

2. Click the **Chart2** tab to view the column chart.

3. Select the **Office Button** and display the **Print** options. Select **Print Preview**. The chart orientation is **Landscape**.

4. Close **Print Preview** and to change the orientation, click the **Orientation** button.

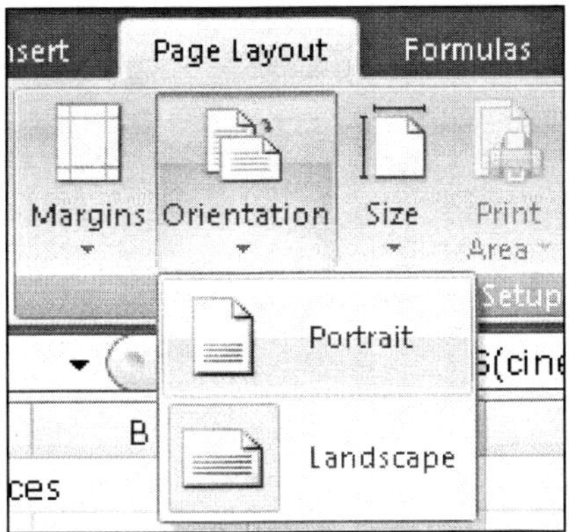

5. Select **Portrait**. This turns the paper vertically.

6. **Print Preview** the chart. The display now shows how the spreadsheet would appear when printed.

Note: *The size of the titles and the legend will change automatically when the orientation is changed.*

7. Print a portrait copy of the chart.

8. Close the workbook <u>without</u> saving.

Exercise 74 - Revision

1. Open the workbook **compdata2** (created in **Exercise 56**).

2. Click on the chart to select it.

3. Move the chart to a sheet named **Pie Chart**.

4. Change the orientation of the chart to **portrait**, as it is required for a report already printed in that format.

5. Add a centred footer **Created by** followed by your name.

6. Print a copy of the **Pie Chart**.

7. Close the workbook <u>without</u> saving the changes.

Exercise 75 - Revision

1. Open the workbook **Population** (created from data in **Exercise 55**).

2. Select the chart and move it to a separate sheet named **Bar**.

3. Check that orientation of the chart is landscape.

4. Add a footer with the date in the left section (either type in the date or use the code button for the date) and your name in the right section.

5. Print two copies of the chart using a single action.

6. Close the workbook <u>without</u> saving.

Section 12

Cell Referencing

By the end of this Section you should be able to:

Use Relative Addressing

Use Absolute Addressing

Use Mixed Cell Referencing

Exercise 76 - Relative Addressing

Guidelines:

As a formula is copied across a range of cells, the formulas change automatically. The calculation is performed on cells in the positions relative to those copied, e.g. **B2+B3** becomes **C2+C3** then **D2+D3**, as the formula is copied from column to column.

The formulas can be copied to any cells in any position on a worksheet.

Actions:

1. Start a new workbook.

2. In cell **B2** enter **7** and in **B3** enter **8**. In cell **B4** create a formula **=B2+B3** to add the two numbers.

3. Click on cell **B4** and click the **Copy** button, . Move to cell **D8** and press **<Enter>** to paste the copy. The result **0** is displayed.

4. The formula is copied and adds the cells relative to the formula, i.e. the two cells directly above. Enter **5** and **3** into cells **D6** and **D7**.

	A	B	C	D	E
1					
2		7			
3		8			
4		15			
5					
6				5	
7				3	
8				8	
9					
10					

5. All formulas copied have been relative whether using **Copy** or the **Fill Handle**.

6. Click on cell **B4** and drag its **Fill Handle** across three columns. The results are displayed as **0**.

7. Examine the formulas in cells **C4**, **D4** and **E4**.

8. Enter numbers into the two cells above the three formulas to test and see if they work.

9. Close the workbook <u>without</u> saving.

Exercise 77 - Absolute Addressing

Guidelines:

Sometimes, a fixed cell address in a formula is required which refers to the same cell when the formula is copied. To stop the formula changing automatically, cell references included in it can be fixed. This is known as absolute addressing or absolute referencing.

To fix a cell as **Absolute**, the **$** symbol must be added to the cell references. The **$** symbol is typed in as the cell reference is written, or the function key **<F4>** may be used after entering a cell reference to change the reference to absolute. Repeated use of the **<F4>** key changes to mixed addressing, e.g. **B15** (relative), **$B$15** (absolute), **B$15** (mixed, fixed row), **$B15** (mixed, fixed column). Mixed addressing is rarely used. Cells may be defined as having absolute columns, rows or, more commonly, both.

Absolute addressing is used to reference fixed costs like standing orders, tax rates, VAT rate, etc.

Actions:

1. Open the workbook **VAT**.

2. Make **B15** the active cell and enter the new **VAT Rate** of **17.5%** (enter as **0.175** or **17.5%**).

3. Move into cell **C6** and enter the formula for the **VAT** (**Price** multiplied by the **VAT Rate**).

4. Drag this formula across into **D6** and **E6**. The resulting **VAT** is **zero**. Check the formulas in **D6** and **E6** to find the problem. It has been caused by relative addressing. The **VAT Rate** is only in one cell (fixed) but the formulas have automatically changed to reference cells that are empty, e.g. the cells **C15** and **D15**.

5. In cell **C6**, enter the formula **=C5*$B$15**. The **$** symbols fix this cell as absolute.

Note: *If the above formula is entered by pointing and clicking on cell **B15**, pressing the **Function** key <F4> immediately after selecting the cell automatically changes the reference to an absolute address.*

6. Copy the formula across the next two columns. View the contents of **D6** to see if the formula still uses **B15** for the **VAT Rate**.

7. Complete the **Total Price** row by adding the **Price** and **VAT**.

8. Save the workbook as **VAT2** and close it.

Exercise 78 - Mixed Referencing

Guidelines:

Mixed Referencing is a combination of between **Absolute** and **Relative**. One part of the reference is fixed with a **$** symbol and the other part is not, e.g. **$A15** (column **A** fixed) or **A$15** (row **15** fixed).

Actions:

1. Start a new workbook and create the following spreadsheet to calculate a table of percentages of the numbers in column **A**.

	A	B	C	D	E	F	G
1							
2		10%	20%	30%	40%	50%	
3	5						
4	10						
5	15						
6	20						
7	25						
8							

2. In cell **B3** enter the formula **=A3*B2**, to calculate **10%** of **5**.

3. Use the **Fill Handle** to drag the formula across to **F3**.

4. With the range still highlighted, drag the **Fill Handle** down to row **7** to fill the rest of the range.

	A	B	C	D	E	F	G
1							
2		10%	20%	30%	40%	50%	
3	5	0.5	0.1	0.03	0.012	0.006	
4	10	5	0.5	0.015	0.00018	1.08E-06	
5	15	75	37.5	0.5625	0.000101	1.09E-10	
6	20	1500	56250	31640.63	3.203613	3.5E-10	
7	25	37500	2.11E+09	6.67E+13	2.14E+14	74902.76	
8							

5. This is obviously not the desired result. Double click on cell **D5** to check the formula and which cells it uses. The formula should be **=A5*D2** but because of **Relative Addressing** it has been copied as **=C5*D4**.

6. Highlight and delete the range **B3:F7**.

7. Try and use **Absolute Referencing** to overcome this problem. In cell **B3** type the formula **=$A$3*$B$2**.

8. Drag this formula across to column **F** and then down to row **7**.

continued over

Exercise 78 - Continued

9.   This is still incorrect. Double click on cell **D5** to check the formulas and which cells it uses. The formula is **=$A$3*$B$2**, so all of the formulas are now exactly the same.

◢	A	B	C	D	E	F	G
1							
2		10%	20%	30%	40%	50%	
3	5	0.5	0.5	0.5	0.5	0.5	
4	10	0.5	0.5	0.5	0.5	0.5	
5	15	0.5	0.5	=$A$3*$B!	0.5	0.5	
6	20	0.5	0.5	0.5	0.5	0.5	
7	25	0.5	0.5	0.5	0.5	0.5	
8							

10.   **Mixed Referencing** must be used to provide the solution. It can fix the column as **A** and row as **2**, allowing the other reference to change as the formula is copied across the range.

11.   Highlight, then delete the range **B3:F7** again and move back to cell **B3**.

12.   Type the formula **=$A3*B$2**, this fixes column **A** and row **2** because the **dollar** signs are before these values in the formula.

13.   Drag this new formula across to **F3** and then down to row **7**.

14.   This is now the expected result. Double click in cell **D5** to confirm that the formula is **=$A5*D$2**.

◢	A	B	C	D	E	F	G
1							
2		10%	20%	30%	40%	50%	
3	5	0.5	1	1.5	2	2.5	
4	10	1	2	3	4	5	
5	15	1.5	3	=$A5*D$2	6	7.5	
6	20	2	4	6	8	10	
7	25	2.5	5	7.5	10	12.5	
8							

15.   Save the workbook as **Mixed** and then close it.

Exercise 79 - Revision

Note: *The answers for this exercise are listed in the **Answer Section** at the end of the guide.*

1. Open the workbook **Company**. The overheads in row **9** have been entered into each cell. Changing the overheads means each cell has to be changed.

2. To set up an absolute reference, in cell **A17** type **Overheads** and in cell **B17** enter **4980**.

3. In row **9** add absolute addressing so that all cells reference cell **B17**.

4. To change the **Overheads** for the entire row, just enter **4850** in **B17**.

5. Using **Print Preview** and **Page Setup** alter the settings to fit the worksheet on one page, centred.

6. Print a copy of the worksheet.

7. Close the workbook <u>without</u> saving.

8. Start a new workbook.

9. Create the worksheet as below, formatting these titles to **Bold** and changing the font size to **12**.

	A	B	C	D	E	F	G
1	Number Square						
2							
3		1	2	3	4	5	
4	1						
5	2						
6	3						
7	4						
8	5						
9							

10. In cell **B4** enter a formula which will multiply cells **A4** and **B3**. What is this formula?

11. Change each of the cell references in the formula to be a mixed cell reference that can be successfully copied across the spreadsheet. What is the formula now?

12. Copy the formula across to column **F** and then down to row **8**.

13. What is the formula is cell **E7**?

14. Save the workbook as **Number Square** and then close it.

Section 13

Functions

By the end of this Section you should be able to:

Understand Functions

Use Insert Function

Use SUM, MAX and MIN

Use COUNT, COUNTA and AVERAGE

Use SUMIF and COUNTIF

Use IF

Exercise 80 - Functions

Guidelines:

Functions are specialised formulas that make calculations easier. There are various types, some examples include:

Statistical	AVERAGE, COUNT, MAX, MIN, STDEV, VAR
Financial	NPV, FV, PMT, RATE, IRR
Logical	IF, TRUE, FALSE
Math & Trig	MOD, SIN, LOG, SQRT
Text	LEFT, RIGHT, MID, LEN
Date & Time	DATE, NOW, TIME
Lookup & Reference	HLOOKUP, VLOOKUP, CHOOSE

These standard functions provide accurate calculations - there is no risk of errors appearing in the formulas. Because of this, it is better to use the functions available than to try and type formulas manually.

All functions, like formulas, are preceded by an = sign.

=SUM(N12:N16) adds the values in the range **N12:N16** and is equivalent to the formula **=N12+N13+N14+N15+N16**. The bigger the range the more effective the function. Extending a formula to add 5000 numbers in a column is just as easy as adding 3 numbers.

The **Formulas** tab includes a **Function Library** which can help you insert formulas easily.

Actions:

1. On a blank worksheet, enter a column of **10** numbers, starting in **B3**.

2. To add the numbers in cell **B13**, type **=Sum(B3:B12)**.

3. Delete **B13** and repeat the function by typing **=Sum(** and then select the range by clicking and dragging **B3:B12**. Finish the formula by typing **)** **<Enter>**.

Note: A different method for entering functions is introduced in the next exercise.

4. Leave this workbook open for the next exercise.

Exercise 81 - Insert Function

Guidelines:

The **Insert Function** is a wizard that helps in the entering of functions.

Actions:

1. Using the workbook created in the last exercise, click on cell **B13** and delete the contents.

2. Click the **Insert Function** button, from the **Function Library** on the **Formulas** tab to display the **Insert Function** dialog box or click 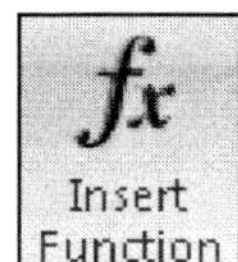 in the **Formula Bar**.

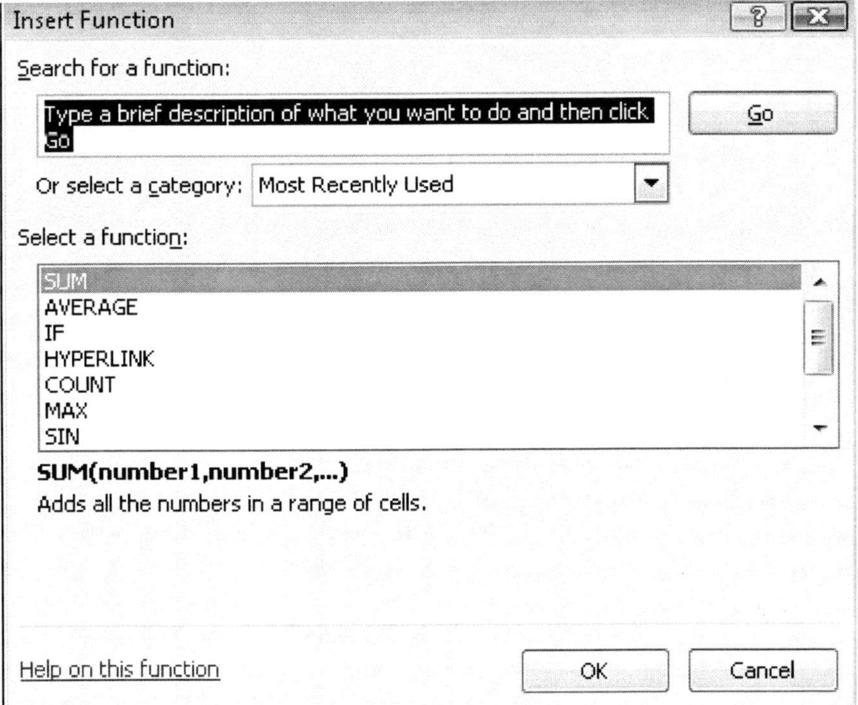

3. Functions can be found using the **Search for a function** box or by selecting a category and then using the **Select a function** box. From the **Or select a category** box select each category in turn to see all available functions - there are well over **200** altogether.

4. Select the category **Math & Trig** from the **Or select a category** drop down list.

5. Scroll down **Select a function** and select **SUM**.

continued over

Exercise 81 - Continued

6. An explanation of the function is given towards the bottom of the box. Click **OK**.

7. The **SUM** box is displayed, prompting for a range to be accepted or selected.

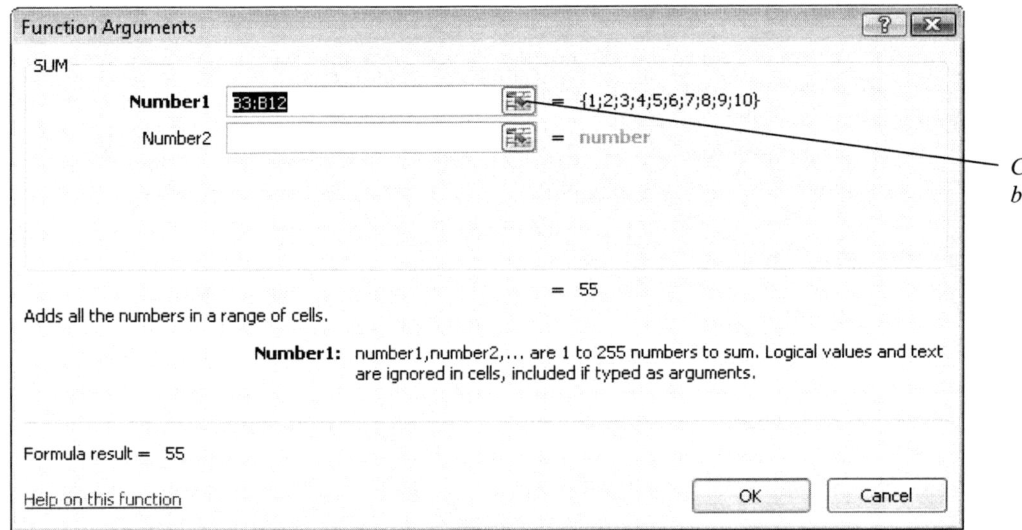

Collapse button

8. The box can be moved around by clicking and dragging on any grey area. Move the box to the right of the screen.

9. To the right of every entry box is a **Collapse** button, that hides most of the box. Click the **Collapse** button of box **Number1**.

10. Click and drag the range **B3:B12** (this is just for practise as the original range was correct).

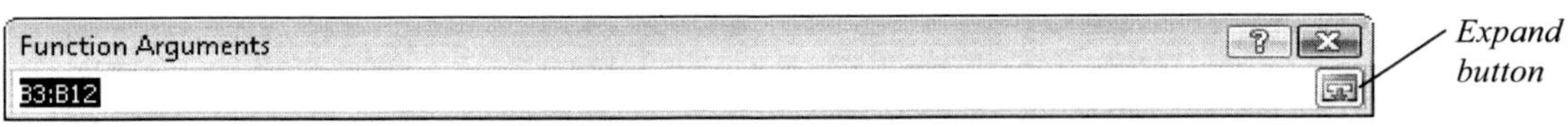

Expand button

11. Click the **Expand** button, (the opposite to **Collapse**).

12. Click **OK**. The function is entered into the worksheet and the result is displayed. All **Functions** can be entered using this method.

13. Close the worksheet <u>without</u> saving.

Exercise 82 - Count, CountA and Average

Guidelines:

Count is a **Function** that counts numeric cells. **CountA** counts the numeric cells as well as cells containing text. **Average** finds the average of a range of numbers.

Actions:

1. Open the worksheet **Numbers**.

2. How many numbers would you say were in this list of numbers on the left of the screen? To find out move to cell **A102** and type **Count**.

3. In cell **B102**, click the **Insert Function** button.

4. Select **Count** from **Most Recently Used, All** or **Statistical** and click **OK**.

5. Type the range **B1:B100** and click **OK**. This displays **99**, the amount of numbers in the range (1 number is missing from the range).

6. Scroll up see why there are only 99 numbers in 100 rows. Fill in the missing row with **23**.

7. Scroll back down to the bottom of the list to see that the count function has been automatically updated and now reads **100**.

8. In cell **A103** type **Average**. In cell **B103**, click the **Insert Function** button.

9. Select **Average** from **Most Recently Used, All** or **Statistical**.

10. Click **OK**.

11. Type the range **B1:B100** and click **OK**. This displays **50**, the average number of the specified range.

Note: *When **Average** or **Count** are used, cells which are blank are ignored, however cells containing zeros are included in the calculations.*

12. Move back to the top of the worksheet and in cell **D11** type **Count** and in **D12** type **CountA**.

13. In **E11** use the **Count** function to count the number of numeric cells in the range **E1:E9**. There are 5.

14. In **E12** use the **CountA** function to count the cells in the range **E1:E9** containing anything. There are 8. Neither function counts the empty cell.

15. Leave the workbook open for the next exercise.

Exercise 83 - Maximum and Minimum

Guidelines:

MAX   finds and displays the largest number in the selected range

MIN   finds and displays the smallest number in the selected range

Actions:

1. The workbook **Numbers** should still be open. If not, open it.

2. In **A104**, enter the text **Max**.

3. With the active cell as **B104**, click the **Insert Function** button.

4. Select **Max** from **Most Recently Used**, **All** or **Statistical**.

5. Click **OK**.

6. Type the range **B1:B100** and click **OK**. This gives the maximum value present in the specified range: **123**.

7. In cell **A105** enter **Min** and in cell **B105** enter the function **=MIN(B1:B100)**. This gives the smallest value: **1**.

8. Change the contents of cell **B100** to **201**. All results of all the functions except **Count** change.

9. Save the workbook as **Numbers2** and close it.

Exercise 84 - IF

Guidelines:

The logical function **IF** compares the contents of a cell and, if a logical test is met, performs one action; if not, it performs another.

=IF(Logical_test,Value_if_true,Value_if_false)

For instance, if the value in cell **A1** is greater than 10 then multiply it by 3, if not, multiply it by 2. This is expressed as: **=IF(A1>10,A1*3,A1*2)**

The **IF** function is sometimes described as **IF THEN ELSE**. **IF** the condition is true **THEN** do this **ELSE** do that.

Actions:

1. On a blank worksheet, enter the label **Interest Calculation** in **B1**.

2. Enter the label **Balance** in cell **B3** and **Interest** in cell **B4**.

3. Enter any number in **C3** for your bank balance.

4. The interest on your money depends on whether the balance is over or under **£100**. Click in cell **C4**, click the **Insert Function** button. Select **IF** from the **Logical** category.

5. Click **OK** and enter the following values for the test parameters, (the sample results will vary depending on your value in **C3**).

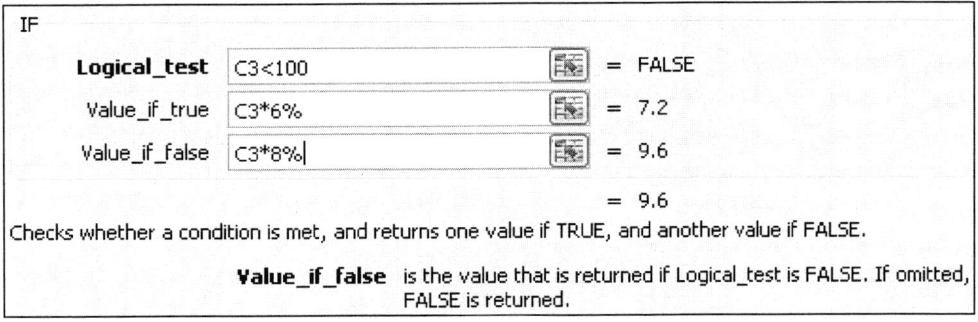

6. Click **OK** to complete the function. The function looks at the contents of cell **C3** and if less than **100**, calculates the interest at **6%** otherwise it calculates it at **8%**.

7. The result of the function, the interest, depends on the balance. Enter **100** in **C3**. The interest is **£8**, (higher rate). Enter **50** and the interest is **£3**, (lower rate). Experiment, change the balance and see the interest change.

8. Close the workbook <u>without</u> saving.

Exercise 85 - CountIF and SumIF

Guidelines:

Countif counts numeric items that match a set condition. **Sumif** only sums values within a range that match a set condition, e.g. to sum the outstanding amount for clients who owe more than £100.

Actions:

1. Open the workbook **Invoice List**.

2. In cell **D16** enter the label **Invoices under £500** and widen column **D** to fit the text.

3. To count the number of outstanding invoices which are less than £500, in cell **E16**, click the **Insert Function** button.

4. Select the category **Statistical** and the function **Countif**. Click **OK**.

5. Select the range **E6:E14**.

6. Set the criteria in the **Criteria** box as **<500**.

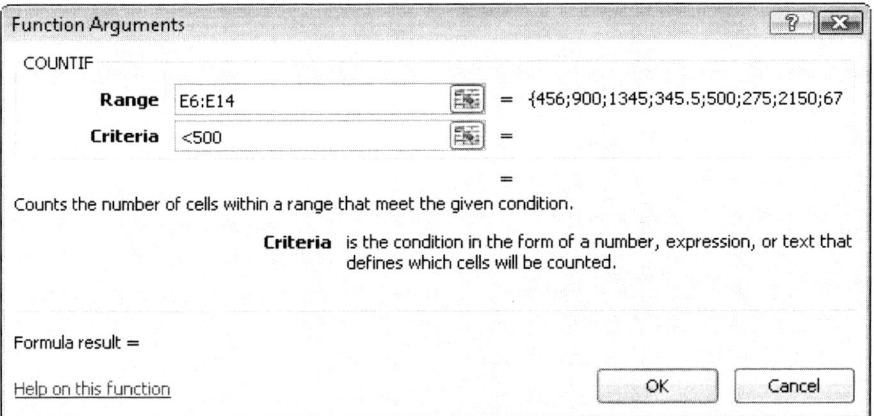

7. Click **OK**. The displayed result is **4**. Check the **Formula Bar** for the formula (the speech marks are added automatically). The cells that match the condition are counted. These cells can also be summed using **Sumif**.

8. In cell **D17**, enter the label **Small invoices total**.

9. In cell **E17** click the **Insert Function** button. Select the **Math & Trig** category and the function **Sumif**. Click **OK**.

10. Select the range **E6:E14** again and set the **Criteria** box to **<500**.

11. Click **OK** to insert the function. The result should be **1454.5**.

12. Close the workbook <u>without</u> saving.

Exercise 86 - Revision

Note: *The answers for this exercise are listed in the **Answer Section** at the end of the guide.*

1. The following data represents sales figures for a group of salespersons. Construct the worksheet and add the data as shown.

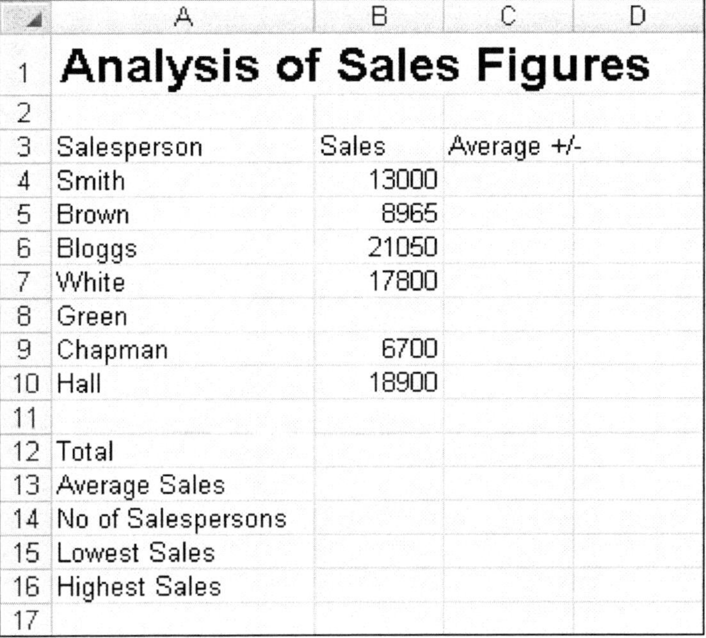

2. Enter the formulas for **Total** and **Average** sales in **B12** and **B13**, using the range **B4:B10**.

3. The number of salespersons is calculated using the **COUNT** function (remember to count the sales figures, not the names).

4. Calculate the highest and lowest sales using the **MAX** and **MIN** functions.

5. The **Average +/-** column is calculated by subtracting the average sales from the individual's sales (remember Absolute and Relative addressing when copying formulas).

6. It is very important to decide whether to enter a zero in cell **B8** or to leave it blank. Add **0** to **B8**. The answers are different.

Note: *This is the part of statistics that can be manipulated one way or another depending on what the results are to convey.*

7. Print a copy of the worksheet.

8. Save the workbook as **Sales Analysis** and close it.

Section 14

Names

By the end of this Section you should be able to:

Use Names
Create Names from Ranges
Paste and Apply Names
Use Names in Formulas
Use Names with Find & Select

Exercise 87 - Using Names

Guidelines:

Names can be used to represent the contents of a cell or a range of cells to make referencing them easier.

Formulas use cell addresses, e.g. **F37**; these have to be traced back to see what they represent. For example, a formula might be **=D34-D67**, where **D34** represents **Income** and **D67** represents **Expenditure**. Using **Names** the same formula would be:

= Income - Expenditure

making it easier for anyone viewing the formula to understand what it is.

After naming a range, the name can be used to display or print the range.

Actions:

1. Open the workbook **VAT**.

2. In **C6** enter the formula to calculate the **VAT**. Remember, this will have to use **Absolute Addressing**. The formula is **=C5*$B$15**.

3. Copy this formula across the row into **D6** and **E6**.

4. Complete the **Total Price** row, adding the **Price** to the **VAT**.

5. Click on cell **B15**, the **VAT Rate**. Enter the new rate of **17.5%** (enter **0.175**).

6. The use of **Names** would make the formulas in this worksheet easier to understand. Click on cell **B15** and display the **Formulas** tab.

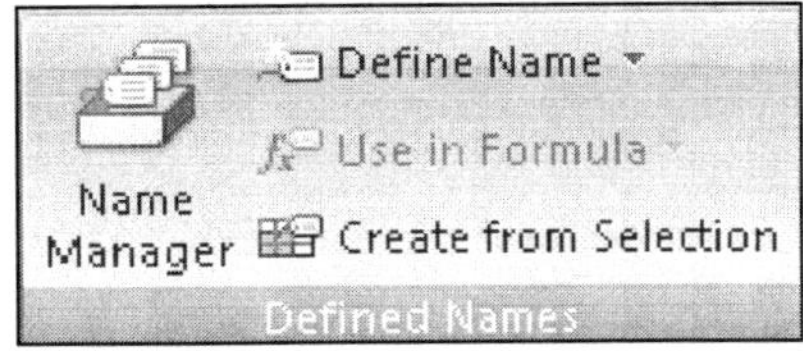

7. Select **Define Name** from the **Defined Names** group.

8. The **New Name** dialog box shows **VAT_Rate** in the **Name** box and where the name **Refers to** (Vat!$B$15). **VAT_Rate** is a suitable name.

continued over

Exercise 87 - Continued

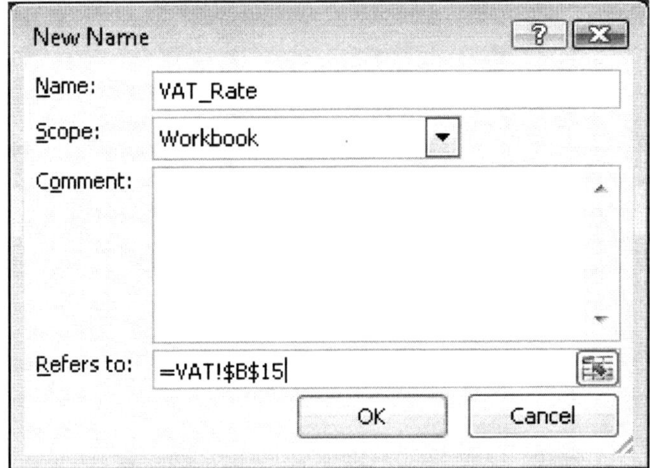

9.   Click **OK** to add this name to the worksheet.

10.   Note that the **Cell Reference Area** now contains the name of the cell, **VAT_Rate** (above the column **A** heading). Move to cell **C6**. The cell contents still reference **$B$15**. The cell has been named but not used anywhere yet.

11.   Click the **Define Name** drop down and select **Apply Names**. A list of available names, in this case just **VAT_Rate** is displayed in the **Apply Names** dialog box.

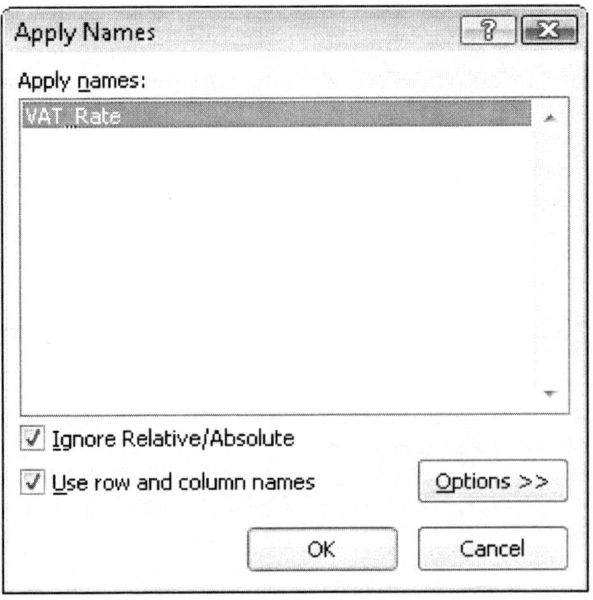

12.   With **VAT_Rate** highlighted, click **OK** to apply this name to any cells referencing this named cell.

13.   Save the workbook as **VAT3** and close it.

Exercise 88 - Create, Paste and Apply Names

Guidelines:

It is possible to create names from row and column titles and then **Paste** or **Apply** the names throughout the worksheet.

Actions:

1. Open the workbook **Budget**.

2. Highlight the whole sheet, i.e. **A1:N14**.

3. To create **Names** from the labels, click **Create from Selection** from the **Defined Names** group.

4. In the **Create Names from Selection** dialog box, ensure that **Top row** and **Left column** are selected.

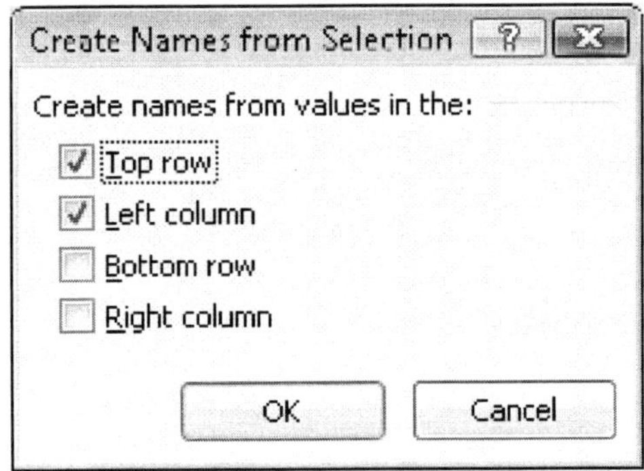

5. Click **OK**.

6. With the data still highlighted, click the **Define Name** drop down and click **Apply Names**.

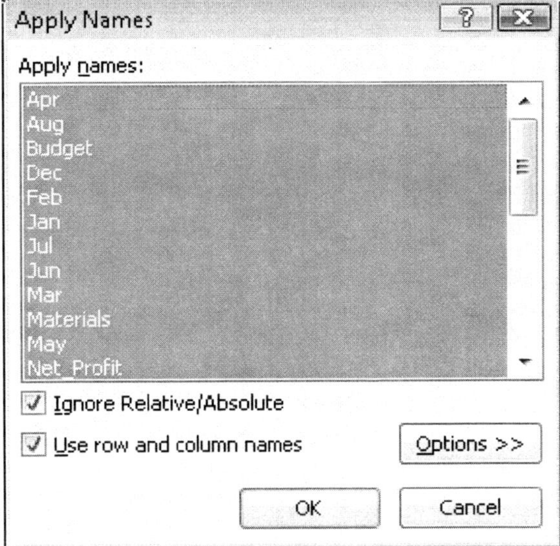

7. The names from the row and column titles are displayed. At this stage names can be deselected by clicking on them. Click **OK** to apply all the names.

8. Browse around the worksheet examining the cell contents, particularly the cells containing calculations. A worksheet containing names is far easier to read and understand than one just using cell references.

9. Save the workbook as **Budget2** and close it.

Exercise 89 - Using Names in Formulas

Guidelines:

Instead of having to type the cell name into a formula, it can be pasted.

Actions:

1. Open the workbook **VAT3** (created as part of **Exercise 87**).

2. Insert a column between **March** and **Total** by highlighting column **F** and right clicking **Insert**. In **F4** enter **April** and in **F5** type **5050** and press **<Enter>**.

3. In **F6** type **=F5*** and then select **Formulas** tab and select **Use in Formula**. Select **VAT_Rate** from the list. The name is pasted into the formula. Press **<Enter>** to complete the formula.

4. Add in the **Total Price** for April.

5. Check the formulas in the **Total** column to make sure that they include the new figures, column **F**, edit if necessary.

6. Leave the workbook open for the next exercise.

Exercise 90 - Using Find and Select with Names

Guidelines:

The **Go To** command can not only be used to move quickly to a cell by typing its reference, but also to move to any named cell or range.

Actions:

1. The workbook **VAT3** should be open from the previous exercise, if not open it.

2. Display the **Home** tab, click **Find & Select** and select **Go To**.

Note: Alternatively the key press <Ctrl G> or the function key <F5> can be used.

3. The names on the sheet are listed, in this case only **VAT_Rate**. Click on **VAT_Rate** and then **OK**.

4. The cell containing the **VAT_Rate**, i.e. **B15**, is now the active cell.

5. Close the workbook <u>without</u> saving.

6. Open the workbook **Budget2** (saved in **Exercise 88**).

7. Press **<F5>**, the **Go To** key. There is now a long list of all the named ranges in this sheet. Select **Materials** then **OK**. The range containing the **Materials** figures will be highlighted. Use the horizontal scroll bar to view the whole range if necessary.

8. Select **Find & Select** and click **Go To**, choose **May** and click **OK**. The figures for **May** are now highlighted.

9. Close the workbook <u>without</u> saving.

Exercise 91 - Revision

*Note: The answers for this exercise are listed in the **Answer Section** at the end of the guide.*

1. Open the workbook **Retail**.

2. Create names for the whole worksheet, i.e. **A1:N14**. Apply these names.

3. Move to cell **P3** and type **=Sales Feb** to find the sales figure for **February**.

4. What is the sales figure for February?

5. Similarly, find the amount of **Spending** in **April (Apr)**, what is the amount?

6. **Go To** the **Sales** figures and make them **bold**.

7. Close the workbook <u>without</u> saving.

Section 15

Linking

By the end of this Section you should be able to:

Create a Link

Link Ranges

Link Open Workbooks

Link Unopened Workbooks

Update Linked Workbooks

Exercise 92 - Linking

Guidelines:

A document link is a formula reference to a cell in another document. The reference is **live**, which means that if referenced sheets are open, the changes are automatically updated, just as they would be if all the data was in the same sheet. The sheet that contains the link is called the **container** document. The documents which include the original data are known as **source** documents.

Links can be used to consolidate several related worksheets into one. For example, information from several sources can be gathered together into one worksheet to show the overall company results from all the divisions. To create links, the source application must support **DDE** (Dynamic Data Exchange) or **OLE** (Object Linking and Embedding).

Linking data has a number of advantages:

- To share information
- To simplify a complex problem by breaking it down into several separate workbooks
- To divide work among several people
- To build models normally too large for memory
- To add flexibility to workbooks

Actions:

1. Close any open workbooks and start a new one.

2. In **A1** enter **Source Workbook**, in cell **B3** enter a number and save the workbook as **Source**.

3. Start a new workbook and in cell **A1** enter **Container Workbook**. Save it as **Container**.

4. To display the two worksheets side by side display the **View** tab and click **Arrange All**.

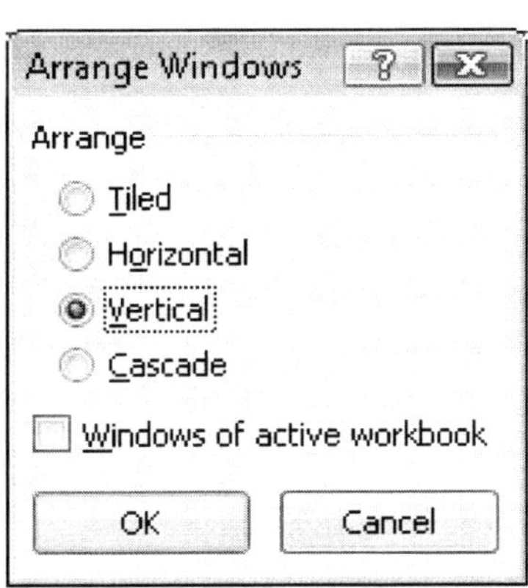

5. Select the **Vertical** option and click **OK**.

6. Make **D5** active (point and click) in **Container**.

7. Create a link by typing **=** and click on cell **B3** in **Source**. Press <Enter> to complete the formula which shows **=[Source.xlsx]Sheet1!$B$3**.

8. In **Source**, change the number in cell **B3**. Cell **D5** in the **Container** worksheet changes automatically because of the link.

9. Leave the two workbooks open for the next exercise.

　　　　　　　　　　　　© CiA Training Ltd 2007

Exercise 93 - Creating Links

Guidelines:

The difference between a worksheet link and a normal cell is that a link reference includes the source workbook and sheet name followed by an **!** e.g. **=[budget.xlsx]Sheet1!C10**. The file specification can include up to 4 parts: drive, path, file name and extension, e.g.

=[C:\EXCEL\DATA\budget.xlsx]Sheet1!B7.

To create a **Link**, copy a selection from the source document and paste into the destination document worksheet using **Paste Special**.

Actions:

1. The workbooks **Source** and **Container** should still be open from the previous exercise. If not, open them.

2. Starting in **B3** in **Source**, enter a list of 5 numbers down the column. Use the **AutoSum** button to total them in **B8**.

3. In cell **D5** in **Container**, type in the label **Total** to overwrite the link from the previous exercise.

4. Make **D6** the active cell in **Container**. Type **=** to start a formula and then point and click twice on **B8** in the **Source** worksheet. Press **<Enter>** to complete the formula. The link is then created and should be **=[Source.xlsx]Sheet1!$B$8**.

5. Copy the contents in cell **B5** in **Source**. Make the workbook **Container** active, click on cell **D8** and click the **Paste** button drop down and select **Paste Special**.

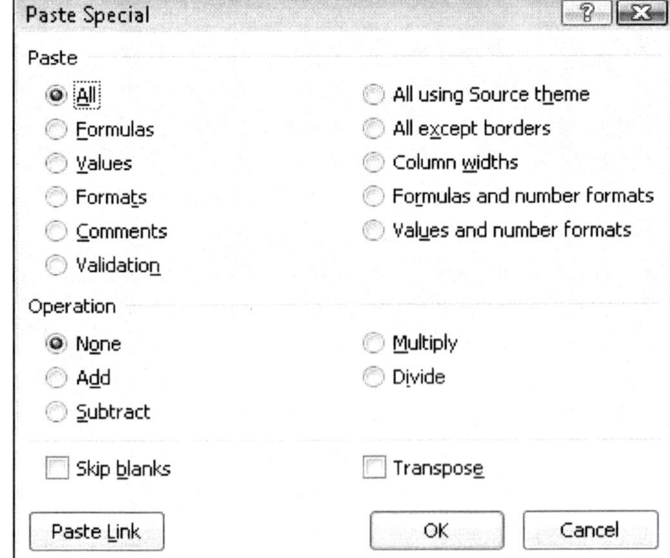

6. Click the **Paste Link** button to create a link. Press **<Esc>** to cancel the marquee.

7. A link has now been created between **B5** in **Source** and **D8** in **Container**. Change the number in **B5**. The numbers in cells **D6** and **D8** in **Container,** and that in **B8** in **Source** change automatically.

8. Leave the two workbooks open for the next exercise.

Exercise 94 - Linking a Range

Guidelines:

Ranges of cells from one worksheet can be linked to another using the **Paste Special** command.

Functions such as **=SUM([sales.xlsx]Sheet1!D1:D50)** can also be used when linking.

Actions:

1. The workbooks **Source** and **Container** should still be open from the previous exercise. If not, open them.

2. In cell **A6** in **Container**, enter the label **Linked Range**. Point and select the range **B3:B7** in **Source**. Select **Copy**.

3. Select **A7** in **Container** and select **Paste Special** from the **Paste** button and click the **Paste Link** button, Paste Link . Press **<Esc>** to cancel the marquee (the dotted line around the original range).

4. The range has been linked as individual cells. Click on cell **A7**, the Formula Bar displays **=[Source.xlsx]Sheet1!B3**. Note that the cell reference is **B3** which is not absolute, as is the case with individually linked cells.

5. Clear the formula from **B8** in **Source** and the link in cell **D6** in **Container**.

6. Make **D6** the active cell in **Container**. Type **=SUM(** and then select the range **B3:B7** in **Source**. Close the bracket **)** and press <**Enter**> to finish the formula.

7. The figures in **Source** are now totalled in cell **D6** in worksheet **Container** and not in **Source**.

8. Save the current positions of the two workbooks, save the **Source** workbook first.

Note: Always save the source documents before saving the destination worksheet linked to them. This ensures that the document names in external references are current.

9. Close the **Container** workbook.

10. Leave the **Source** workbook open for the next exercise and maximise it.

Exercise 95 - Updating Linked Workbooks

Guidelines:

Links can be maintained to documents that are not open, as long as the container document has access to the source document/s (within the same system, network or disk). If the source documents are not open, the linked references include the drive and pathname, e.g.

[C:\Excel\Data\tax.xlsx]Sheet1!$A$1

whereas, if open, the reference would be **=[tax.xlsx]Sheet1!$A$1**.

Actions:

1. The workbook **Source** should still be open, if not, open it.

2. Change any of the five numbers in column **B**.

3. Remember the changes to the data. Save and close **Source**.

4. Open **Container**. If you receive a message about links, click the **Options** button, select **the Enable this content** and click **OK**. The links are updated and the new numbers are displayed.

5. Save and close the **Container** Workbook.

6. Open the **Source** Workbook.

7. Change the number in cell **B3** in **Source** to **1000**. Save and close the **Source** workbook.

8. Open the container document **Container**.

9. The links are not updated automatically. The contents of cell **A7** still shows the previous value and not **1000**.

10. The links can be updated at any time, Click **Options** on the **Security Warning** line, choose **Enable this content** and click **OK**.

11. The links have now been updated. Cell **A7** displays **1000**.

12. Save and close the **Container** workbook.

Exercise 96 - Revision

1. Make sure that there are no workbooks open, even a blank workbook. Open the workbooks **Hotel2003**, **Hotel2004**, and **Hotel2005**.

2. The occupancy figures for single rooms are to be compared over the three year period. Open **Hotel Library**.

3. The single room bookings are all stored in **B7:M7** of the 3 source workbooks. The ranges to copy have all been named **singles**. Create the necessary links to **Hotel Library**.

4. Make the **Hotel Library** workbook active and maximise the window. Enter the formulas to calculate % occupancy in the rows **10** to **12**, assume a **300** room per month capacity (rooms/300).

5. Format the range **B10:M12** as percentages to two decimal places.

6. Calculate the total of the rows **6** to **8** in column **N**.

7. Calculate the average occupancy on rows **10** to **12** in column **N**.

8. Use **Page Setup** and **Print Preview** to set the **Hotel Library** worksheet to print on one piece of paper, landscape. Print a copy of the worksheet.

9. Save the workbook as **Hotel Occupancy**.

10. Close all the open workbooks <u>without</u> saving.

      © CiA Training Ltd 2007

Section 16

Filtering and Sorting

By the end of this Section you should be able to:

Use AutoFilter on a List

Sort Data

Sort a List

Exercise 97 - Creating a List

Guidelines:

Enter the **Column** names (**Fields**) as labels across a row. The data is entered directly below them, following these rules:

- The area to be used must be rectangular, although it may contain blanks.

- Use the same type of data in each column.

- Do not separate the labels from the data with a blank or decorative row.

- Do not duplicate column names and to avoid confusion they should be different from any range names.

- Enter all the list information across each row.

Actions:

1. In a new workbook, enter the list information as shown in the rows and columns below:

	A	B	C	D	E
1					
2					
3	Item	Classification	Price	Sold Today?	
4	Whole milk	Dairy	0.89	Yes	
5	Butter	Dairy	0.95	Yes	
6	Basmati Rice	Provisions	1.39	Yes	
7	Cauliflower	Fruit and veg	0.25	Yes	
8	Pizza	Frozen	2.99	Yes	
9	Country ham	Delicatessen	0.75	No	
10	Gorgonzola	Delicatessen	1.75	No	
11	Semi-skimmed milk	Dairy	0.89	Yes	
12	Guinness	Wines and Spirits	4.95	No	
13	Weetabix (24)	Provisions	1.26	No	
14	Crisps (6)	Provisions	0.99	Yes	
15	Coffee	Provisions	2.45	Yes	
16	Bananas	Fruit and veg	1.29	Yes	
17	Beaujolais	Wines and Spirits	3.25	Yes	
18	Yogurt	Dairy	1.25	No	
19					

2. Save the workbook as **Corner shop**.

3. Close the workbook.

Exercise 98 - Filtering Lists

Guidelines:

Filtering is a quick way to find records in a list that match search criteria. Only the rows that match are displayed. The rows that do not match are hidden.

There are two ways to filter a list: the **AutoFilter** (for a simple filter) and the **Custom Filter** (for more complex filtering). When a list is filtered, the worksheet is placed in **Filter Mode**.

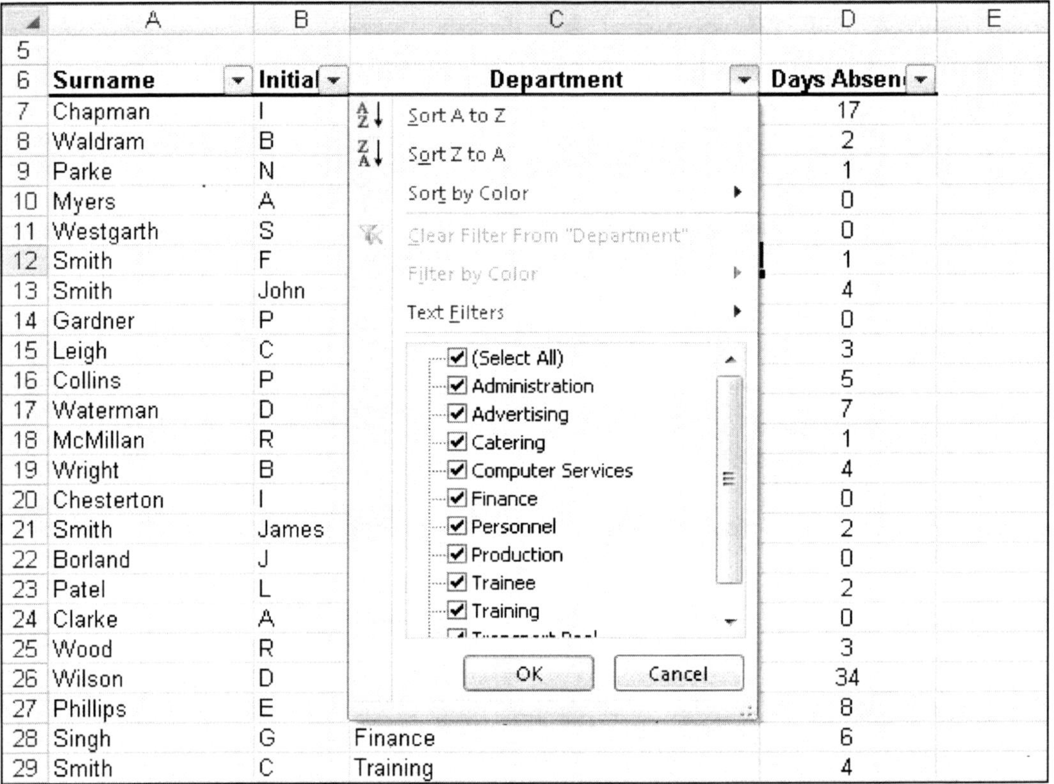

A worksheet in Filter Mode

In **Filter Mode**, the labels at the top of the list contain drop down arrows. If one of these arrows is clicked, a list of all items in the column is revealed. The filter to be applied can then be selected from the list.

The default view is to show all rows **(All)**, until an alternative selection is made from the list. Other options include:

Sort A to Z to sort the list into ascending order

Sort Z to A to sort the list into descending order

Text Filters, where two criteria can be applied and data can be compared.

In the example above, all members of staff in the **Training** department can be displayed by selecting **Training** from the drop down list for **Department**.

Exercise 99 - AutoFilter

Guidelines:

AutoFilter produces a subset of a list with the click of a button. This places the worksheet in **Filter Mode**. Click on any of the arrows to display a drop down list of unique items in that column. Click on any item and the matching records (rows) will be displayed with the other rows hidden.

AutoFilter always selects from the whole list. **AutoFilter** can be applied to selected columns in a list by selecting them before entering **Filter Mode**.

Actions:

1. Open the workbook **Sick** and enter **Filter Mode** by clicking on a cell in the list and then selecting **Filter** from the **Data** tab.

2. Using the **Surname** drop down list, click **Select All** to remove all checked items. Scroll down the list and check **Smith**. Click **OK**. Only the Smiths are displayed.

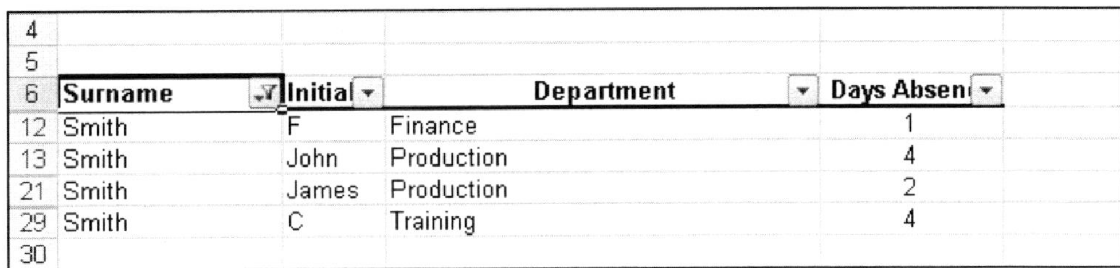

	Surname	Initial	Department	Days Absent
4				
5				
6	Surname	Initial	Department	Days Absent
12	Smith	F	Finance	1
13	Smith	John	Production	4
21	Smith	James	Production	2
29	Smith	C	Training	4
30				

Note: A filtered list can be printed.

3. To redisplay the full list using the **Surname** drop down list, select the **Filters** button from **Surname** and select **Clear Filter from Surname.**

4. Exit **Filter Mode** by clicking the **Filter** button again.

5. Open the workbook **Survey**.

6. Click in the list and enter **Filter Mode**.

7. To display all the males from Sunderland who have replied, select **M** from **Sex**, **Sunderland** from **Town** and **1** from **Reply**.

Note: The drop down arrows are replaced with a filter symbol, if active.

8. To redisplay the whole list, instead of selecting **All** from the three lists, click the **Filter** button.

9. Close the workbook **Survey** <u>without</u> saving.

10. Leave the workbook **Sick** open for the next exercise.

Exercise 100 - Custom AutoFilter

Guidelines:

Custom AutoFilter allows more complicated details than a simple information match. Two items within the same column can be searched for using any of the 12 options (equals, is less than, etc.).

Actions:

1. The workbook **Sick** should still be open. If not, open it.

2. Place the active cell inside the list and to enter filter mode, click the **Filter** button on the **Data** tab.

3. Click the **Filter** drop down from **Days Absence**, select **Number Filters** and then **Less than**.

*Note: Simple searches can be carried out using one set of criteria. More complicated filters can be carried out using either **And** or **Or** to then add another set of criteria.*

4. To display all the employees who have had less than five days absence, **is less than** is displayed in the **Days Absent** box, enter **5** in the **Information** box.

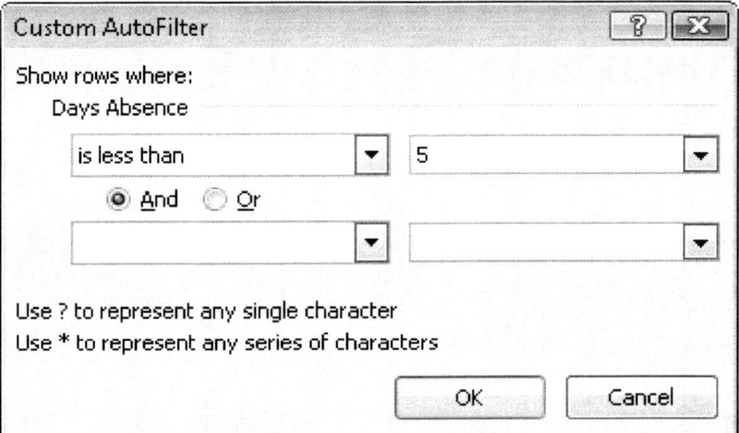

5. Click **OK**.

6. To restore the list, click on the **Days Absence** field drop down list and check **Select All** and click **OK**.

7. To display all the employees in either the **Administration** or **Computer Services** departments, click the **Filter** drop down from **Department**.

8. Select **Text Filters** and **Custom Filter**, use **equals** and the **Or** option.

continued over

Exercise 100 - Continued

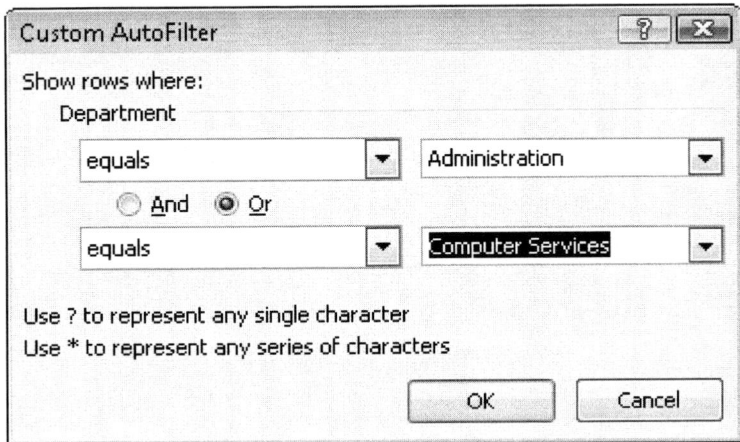

9.   Click **OK** to complete the filter.

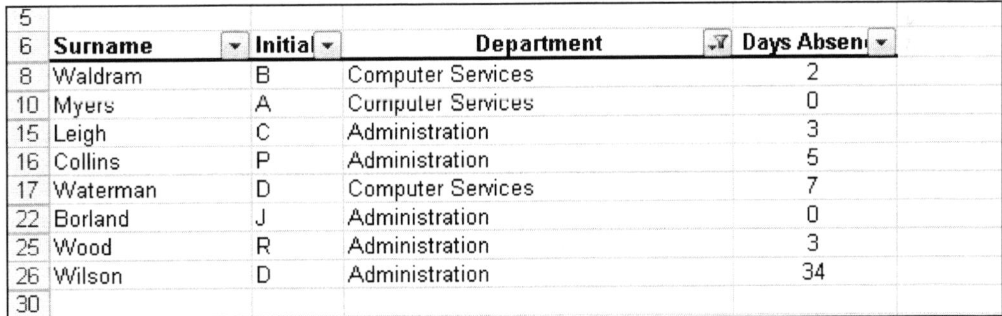

10.   Exit **Filter Mode** by clicking the **Filter** again.

Note: *An alternative is to display the **Home** tab, click the **Sort & Filter** button in the **Editing** group, then **Filter**.*

11.   Close the workbook <u>without</u> saving.

Exercise 101 - Sorting

Guidelines:

Ranges of cells in a worksheet can be sorted so that the rows in the range are arranged in a specific order. The column used to control the sort is called the **Sort Key**. The **Sort** buttons are available from two **Ribbon** tabs, the **Home** tab via the **Sort & Filter** button and the **Data** tab in the **Sort & Filter** group.

Actions:

1. Start a new workbook.

2. Enter a column of 8 names (surnames or first names) starting in cell **B3**.

3. Sort the names into ascending alphabetic order by highlighting the range to be sorted (**B3:B10**) and clicking the **Sort A to Z** button, from the **Sort & Filter** group on the **Data** tab.

Note: *Selecting the range to be sorted is not strictly necessary in this example, but it shows the technique of sorting cells that may be part of a larger spreadsheet.*

4. With the range still selected, click the **Sort Z to A** button, .

5. Add some ages (in years) in column **C** adjacent to each of the names.

6. To sort all of the data in ascending order of age, highlight the range **B3:C10** and click the **Sort** button.

7. In the first **Sort** box select **Column C** and change the sort to ascending, select **Smallest to Largest** from the **Order** drop down.

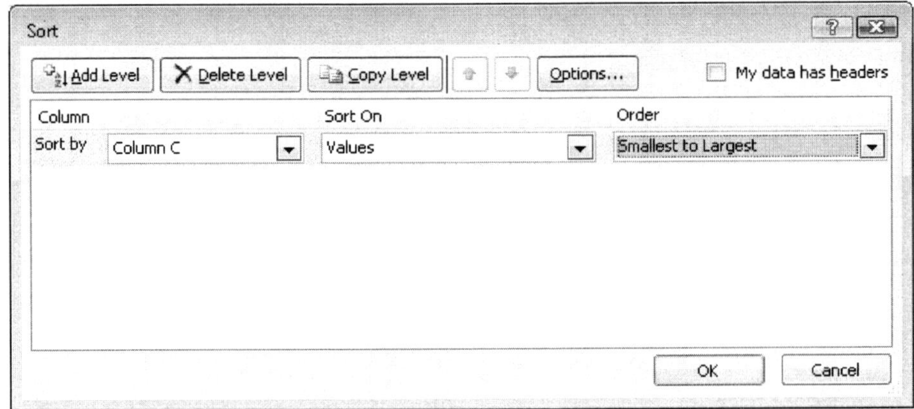

8. Click **OK** to perform the sort.

9. Close the workbook <u>without</u> saving.

Note: *Columns can be sorted by selecting the **Options** button within **Sort** and choosing the **Sort left to right** option.*

Exercise 102 - Sorting a List

Guidelines:

In a list, the records (rows) can be sorted based on the values of one or more of the fields (columns). To sort a list, the method is the same as for an ordinary sort, except that the data does not have to be selected prior to sorting. Selecting any cell in the list will automatically sort the whole list.

The **Sort A to Z** and **Sort Z to A** buttons can still be used for sorting columns of text. When sorting numbers the buttons change to **Sort Smallest to Largest** and **Sort Largest to Smallest**.

Actions:

1. Open the workbook **Cars**.

2. To sort the list into ascending order by **Make** and a secondary sort by **Model**, move the active cell into the column under **Make** and click the **Sort** button.

3. The list is defined as having a header row, **My data has headers** is checked.

4. Under **Column** select **Make** in the **Sort by** box. Leave **A to Z** selected.

5. Select **Add Level** and select **Model** in the **Then by** box. Leave **A to Z** selected.

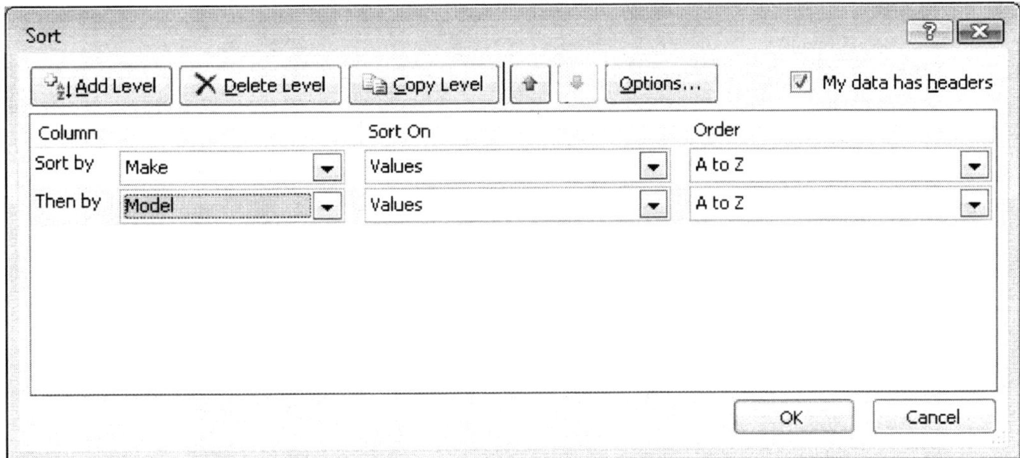

6. Click **OK** to perform the sort.

7. Select **Undo** to return the list to the original order.

continued over

Exercise 102 - Continued

8. Insert a new **Column A** and set the column width to **3.00** units.

9. Label the column **No** in cell **A1**. Number each row in column **A**, starting in cell **A2**, e.g. **1**, **2**, **3** etc.

10. Sort by **Price** in **descending** order. Which car is the second cheapest?

11. Sort the cars into ascending numeric order by **Mileage**. Which car has the most mileage?

12. Using column **A**, re-sort the range back to its original order.

Note: Leading zeros may have to be added to labels that include numbers so that they sort correctly.

13. Save the workbook as **Cars2** and close it.

*Note: The answers for this exercise are listed in the **Answer Section** at the end of the guide.*

Exercise 103 - Revision

1. Open the workbook **League**.

2. Sort the teams into alphabetic name order.

3. **Undo** the last operation.

4. Sort the teams into descending order of points. If the points are equal, then sort on the greater goal difference - if this is the same, again in descending order. Then sort on **For** (descending).

5. Print a copy of the **League Table**.

6. Close the workbook <u>without</u> saving.

Exercise 104 - Revision

1. Open the workbook **Staff**.

2. Display the **AutoFilter** and filter the list to display only the employees in the **Computer Services** department.

3. Display all the records.

4. Filter the list to show the employees between **40** and **50** years old inclusive.

5. Print a copy of the filtered list.

6. Remove the **AutoFilter**.

7. Close the workbook <u>without</u> saving.

Answers

Exercise 22

Step 3 - **98,740**

Step 4 - **61,624**

Step 7 - **59,868**

Step 8 - **34,297**

Step 9 - **246,074**

Exercise 28

Step 7 - **83,877**

Exercise 56

Step 8   Cambridge

Exercise 57

Step 6   March

Exercise 59

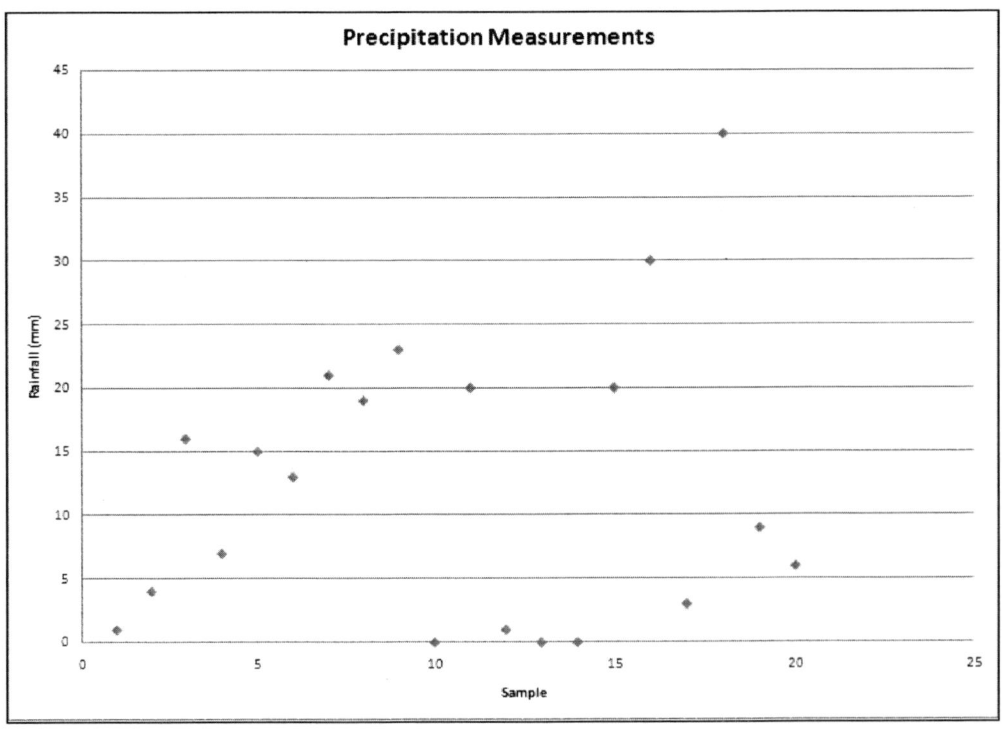

Exercise 60

Step 1	Insert tab and select chart type from the **Charts group**
Step 2	Selecting Insert **tab**
Step 3	Before. Sometimes the data is selected automatically. Otherwise the data has to be selected using the **Select Data** button.
Step 4	**Column**, **Line** and **Pie**
Step 5	**Bar**, **XY Scatter** and **Line - Column**
Step 6	**Line** chart
Step 7	**XY Scatter** chart
Step 8	**Line** or **Column** chart
Step 9	**XY Scatter** chart
Step 10	**Pie** chart
Step 11	**Column** chart the data is represented by vertical columns and a **Bar** chart displays horizontal bars. The two axes change places.

Exercise 66

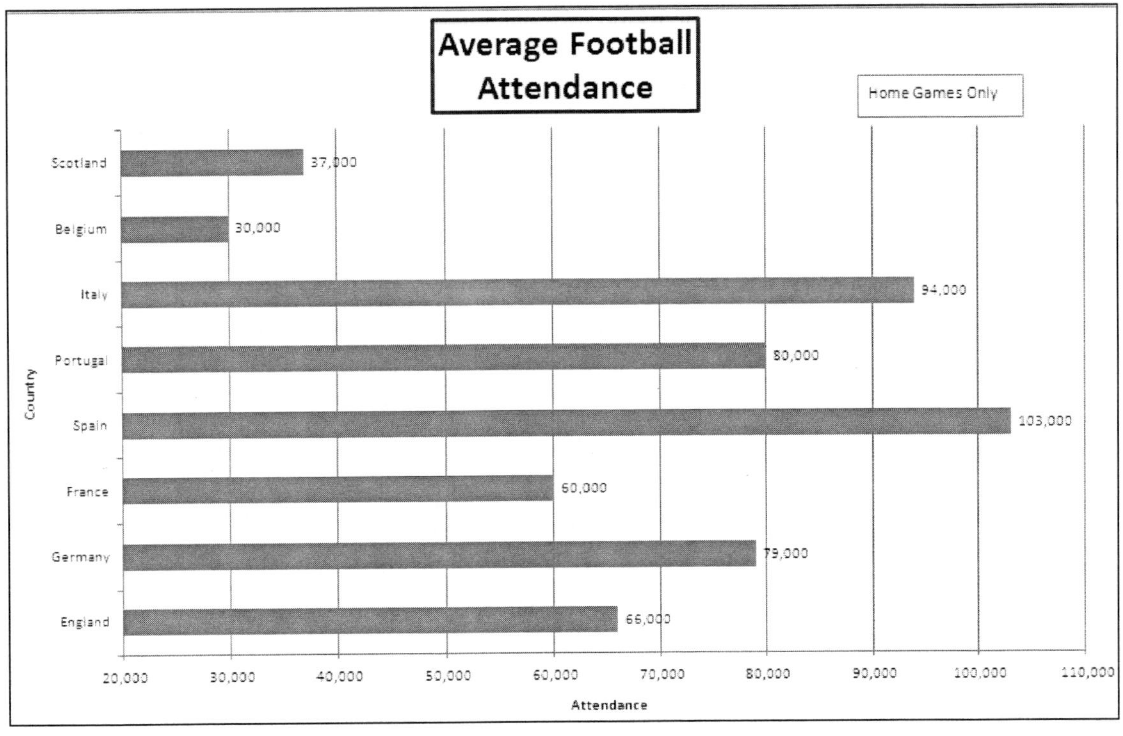

Exercise 67

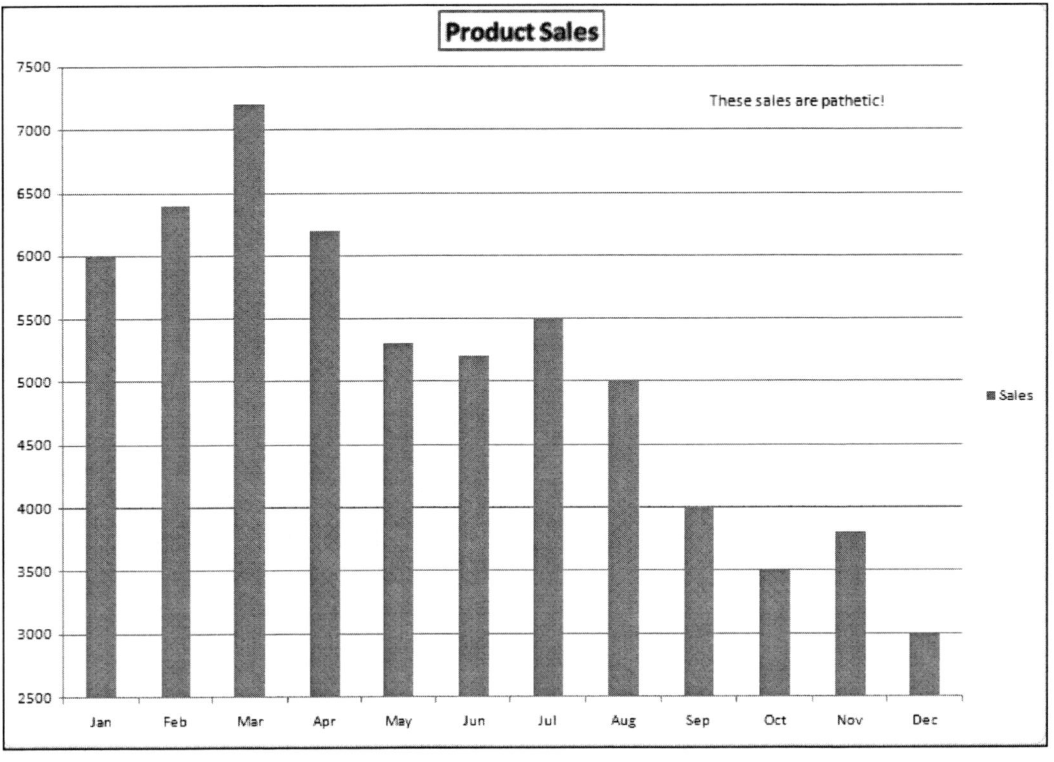

Exercise 69

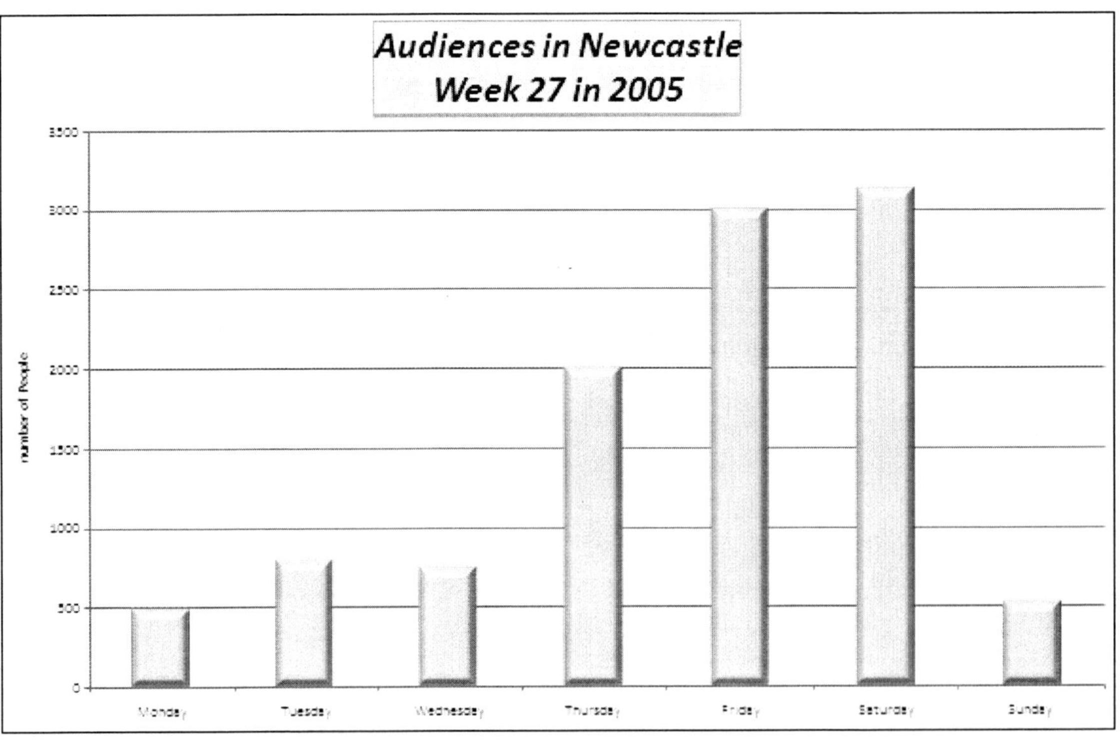

Exercise 71

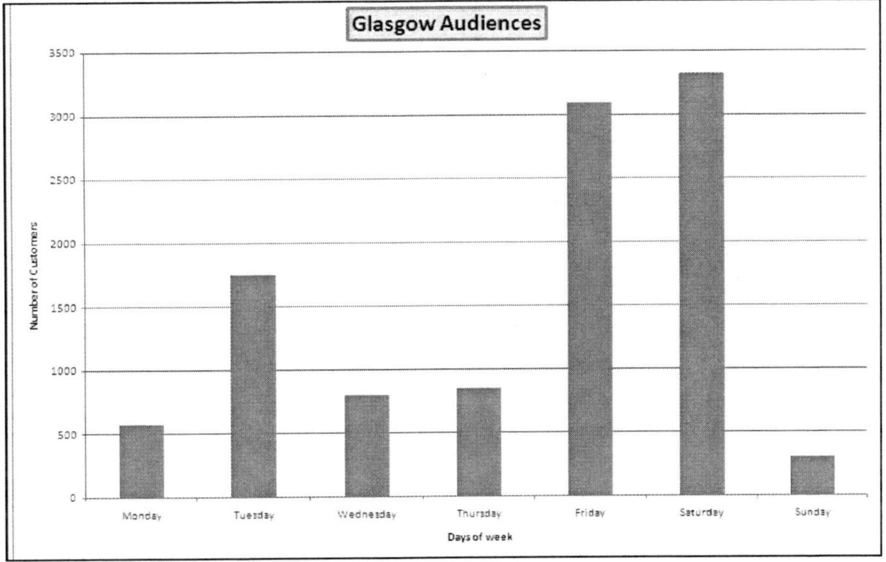

Exercise 79

Step 11 - **=A4*B3**

Step 12 - **=$A4*B$3**

Step 14 - **=$A7*E$3**

Exercise 86

Step 2 - Total is **86415**, Average is **14402.5**

Step 3 - Count is **6**

Step 4 - Min is **6700**, Max is **21050**

Step 6 - When **0** is added to the list the answers that change are: Average **12345**, Count **7** and Min **0**.

Exercise 91

Step 4 - **2000**

Step 5 - **12720**

Exercise 102

Step 8 - **Ford Escort L342 PUK**

Step 9 - **Fiat 126**

Glossary

Active Cell	The currently selected cell in a spreadsheet
Addressing	A method of referencing cells, relative, absolute or mixed.
Alignment	The position of data in a cell. For chart labels, this is the angle at which relevant text is displayed
AutoSum	A function to sum a range of numbers
Average	Function that adds a range and divides the number of numbers
BODMAS	The order in which calculations are performed in a formula
Border	The edge of a cell or range, type and colour of line
Category Axis	Horizontal (X) axis of a chart (vertical for bar charts)
Cell	The smallest part of a spreadsheet, the intersection of one row and one column
Chart	A pictorial representation of numerical data
Chart Area	The area of a worksheet containing the whole chart, which can be moved and resized
Count	Function that displays the number of numbers in a range
Data Series	The values that make up one 'set' of data on a chart
Delete	To erase the contents of a selected cell or range
Embedded	A term that describes any object (e.g. chart) placed on a worksheet, that can be selected, resized or moved
Excel	*Microsoft's* spreadsheet application software
Fill Handle	A cursor used to copy data
Font	A type or style of text
Footer	Information appearing on the bottom of every printed page
Format	Changing the appearance of information
Formula	A calculation, can use values and/or cell references

Formula Bar	A bar above the main worksheet area that displays the actual content of the active cell
Function	Specialised formulas that make calculations easier
Gridlines	On a chart these are lines in the data area showing the position of certain interval markers on the axes
Header	Information appearing on the top of every printed page
House style	Rules set by an organisation that govern the appearance of all of their documents
IF	Logical function that a carries out a test and performs one action if true and another if false
Importing	Transferring data into a spreadsheet from an external source
Label	Text entries that describe the contents of areas of the chart or worksheet e.g. titles, legends, column/row titles
Legend	A key that identifies the patterns or colours assigned to each data series in a chart
Maximum	Function that displays the largest number in a range
Minimum	Function that displays the smallest number in a range
Pixel	Individual small squares that make up a screen display
Plot Area	The area of a chart containing all of the plotted data
Range	A group of adjacent cells
Text Box	A frame containing text that allows labels to be displayed on charts and graphs.
Walls	The area of a 3D column chart forming the back and sides of the plot area
Value Axis	Vertical (Y) axis of a chart (horizontal for bar charts)
Workbook	A spreadsheet file
Worksheet	A single page within a workbook

Index

Record of Achievement Matrix

This Matrix is to be used to measure your progress while working through the guide. This is a self assessment process, you judge when you are competent. Remember that afterwards there is an assessment to test your competence.

Tick boxes are provided for each feature. 1 is for no knowledge, 2 is for some knowledge and 3 is for competent. A section is only complete when column 3 is completed for all parts of the section.

Excel 2007 CLAIT Plus

Tick the Relevant Boxes **1**: No Knowledge **2**: Some Knowledge **3**: Competent

Section	No	Exercise	1	2	3
1 Creating a Spreadsheet	1	Spreadsheet Structure			
	2	Creating a Spreadsheet			
	3	Entering Labels			
	4	Entering Numbers			
	5	Saving a New Workbook			
	6	Closing a Workbook			
2 Opening and Importing	8	Opening a Workbook			
	9	Importing Data			
	10	Saving in Different Formats			
3 Formulas	12	Introducing Formulas			
	13	Mathematical Operators			
	14	Brackets			
	15	Selecting Cells With The Mouse			
	16	Percentages			
	17	Ranges			
	18	AutoSum			
	19	Copy and Paste			
	20	Using the Fill Handle			
	21	Checking Formulas			
4 Editing Cells	23	Overtyping			
	24	Deleting Cell Contents			
	25	Undo and Redo			
	26	Editing Data in the Formula Bar			
	27	In Cell Editing			
5 Printing	29	Printing			
	30	Print Preview			
	31	Page Setup			
	32	Portrait and Landscape			
	33	Margins			
	34	Display and Print Formulas			
	35	Gridlines			
	36	Headers and Footers			
	37	Printing a Selection			

Other Products from CiA Training

CiA Training is a leading publishing company, which has consistently delivered the highest quality products since 1985. A wide range of flexible and easy to use self teach resources has been developed by CiA's experienced publishing team to aid the learning process. These include the following materials at the time of publication of this product:

- **Open Learning Guides**

- **ECDL/ICDL & ECDL/ICDL Advanced (ECDL Foundation Qualification)**

- **New CLAIT, CLAIT Plus & CLAIT Advanced (OCR Qualification)**

- **CiA Revision Series**

- **ITQs (Industry Standard Qualification)**

- **e-Citizen (ECDL Foundation Qualification)**

- **Trainer's Packs with iCourse**

- **Start IT (City & Guilds Qualification)**

- **Skill for Life in ICT (Industry Standard Qualification)**

- **iCourse - Course customising software**

We hope you have enjoyed using our materials and would love to hear your opinions about them. If you'd like to give us some feedback, please go to:

www.ciatraining.co.uk/feedback.php

and let us know what you think.

New products are constantly being developed. For up to the minute information on our products, to view our full range, to find out more, or to be added to our mailing list, visit:

www.ciatraining.co.uk